Welcome…

WEAR YOUR KROWN

*The Seven Jewels for
Building Kings & Queens*

**Onassis Krown
Lateef Terrell Warnick**

Audiobook: 978-1-939199-05-8
Paperback: 978-1-939199-15-7
Hardback: 978-1-939199-18-8
eBook: 978-1-939199-23-2
Library of Congress Number: 2023912015

WEAR YOUR KROWN – *The Seven Jewels for Building Kings & Queens*

1. Self-Help 2. Body, Mind & Spirit 3. Self-Improvement 4. Non-Fiction 5. Krown, Onassis 6. Lateef Warnick I. Title

Printed in the United States of America

"Embrace your inner royalty & ignite the flame within. Unleash your limitless potential, for you are a majestic being, crowned in body, mind & spirit. With unwavering determination, honor your journey, and let your light shine with regal grace, for you were born to reign in the kingdom of your making."

Onassis Krown LLC
"Building Kings & Queens!" | WEAR YOUR KROWN?!
www.onassiskrown.com
"If you like the finer things in life… it's OK!"

Your reviews are very important to the work we do. A portion of your proceeds goes to support those suffering from substance abuse and victims of domestic violence. If you share our sentiment, then please take a moment to leave a positive review on Amazon and/or share on your social media outlets. Blessings!

CONTENTS

WEAR YOUR KROWN:
The Seven Jewels for Building Kings & Queens

FOREWARD

Across America and the world at large, many people believe our education systems are failing us. Some believe it is intentional. Some believe in a conspiracy theory that there are "powers that be" who don't want the masses being educated in the truly important life skills that will help them be successful. Many believe our education system is antiquated and designed to create "worker bees" who simply get enough book knowledge to be a good employee but not enough to create wealth, so they'll simply be a pawn for the corporations and the wealthy.

I don't personally know if this conspiracy theory is true or not, but I do agree that our education system across many states is insufficient. I know this firsthand as someone who attained a bachelor's degree in my lifetime but as well as the father of four and someone who taught 7th grade math & science. Students receive inadequate lessons in subjects most have no interest in, won't help them build a quality life and receive information most will never use in their lifetimes. On top of that, many school systems put a ton of focus on End of Grade tests which we all know, not all kids perform well on tests, but they also spend the entire school year building up to the exams which leads to stress and anxiety for many.

Lastly, a lot of school systems have bonus structures that benefit administrators and teachers based on the performance of the students which minimally has led to corruption of these same faculty in the past. So, while this book will not solve all of these problems, I did write it as a tool for readers to use to learn the essential skills not only to create a better quality of life but also to hopefully build character as well as individuals that are better contributors to a more advanced society. School systems are designed to provide basic skills and education, but it is the responsibility of parents, guardians and, unfortunately, the students themselves to proactively get the knowledge they need to live the lives they truly desire. As opposed to simply teaching people how to selfishly "get ahead," I feel it is important to try to help mold and shape people to be the best people they can be that also benefits the masses at large. Hence, I created these Seven Jewels to hopefully help achieve that goal. They are: 1. Financial Wellness 2. Asset Ownership 3. Healthy Living 4. Strategic Education 5. Family 6. Spiritual Growth and 7. Paying it Forward.

Before I even knew what a "Renaissance Man" was, I had friends calling me that. I guess I have always had a thirst for knowledge in many areas and I have worked in many fields over 30+ the years as a Serial Entrepreneur, Naval Officer, Nuclear Engineer, Student Pilot, Financial Advisor, Insurance Agent, Educator, Realtor, Real Estate Investor, Top Sales Professional, Trainer & Manager, Investment Supervision Principal, Hip-Hop Artist, Songwriter, Producer, Independent Record Label Owner, Web Designer, eCommerce Expert, Fashion Designer, Clothing Brand Owner, Online Marketer, Content Creator, Certified Life Coach, Marriage Counselor, Business Consultant, Spiritual Author, Yogi, Husband and Father of four!

In my role as CEO of Onassis Krown, a streetwear brand, I wanted to not just create a brand story but a lifestyle movement for creating "Kings & Queens" in body mind spirit. More than transforming wardrobes, I want to help transform individuals.

My hope is that individuals will read this many times over and use it as a point of reference to come back to time and time again. I hope those individuals learn the material like the back of their hands and become able to share information by word of mouth to others. I hope those individuals share the reading with their spouses and it leads to in depth discussion and a blueprint for couples to build better lives together. I hope as couples become more knowledgeable that they begin to have round table discussions with their children, encouraging their kids to incorporate its ideals, helping to prepare them for adulthood and the world at large. Perhaps in time when individuals start to see themselves as their best versions and set high bars for them to aspire to that in a generations' time, we begin to create a more ideal society that looks past skin color and nationality and look more at the character of a person and see them as a reflection of themselves either at a point in their past or a point in their future.

Scripture tells us "For where two or three are gathered together in my name, there am I in the midst of them." Spouses have a unique opportunity to work together and build a great life together. Part of the problem, however, is many people can be self-centered and forget what made them want to be with someone they loved in the first place. Many people who may achieve a certain level of success have their egos start to get the best of them and they begin to believe they did it all by themselves. Marriage and relationships are hard work though. It takes a certain level of humility, vulnerability, accountability and a willingness to learn. I see a lot of men who want to be treated royally like "Kings" but don't want the other responsibilities that may come along with it. Many women may want to be treated like "Queens" but likewise get caught up in what seems to be the easy way to success in our times and fail to conduct themselves as nobility and dignity should. But if you got two people who may not be perfect and yet are making the effort, being patient and are open to growing into the best versions of themselves then they can become a power couple, create a family and change the trajectory of their lineage for generations to come! Hopefully, this book will be a tool and guidebook to assist in that journey. Maybe one day we'll all live as "Kings & Queens" not seeking dominion over others but simply to have a strict discipline over ourselves while sharing a common interest to help uplift others and make the world a kingdom of Spirit and a place for all!

THE SYMBOLISM OF A CROWN

A royal crown is a powerful symbol that represents authority, power, and sovereignty. It has been used throughout history to denote the highest rank and status of a monarch or ruler. From the ancient Egyptians of Kemet to Europe, Asia and the Americas, royal figures have worn crowns or headdress to denote their status. The symbolism of a royal crown can vary across different cultures and time periods, but there are some common themes associated with it. When we refer to someone as "King" or "Queen," we do not mean dominion over others but rather dominion of oneself. We believe each person is symbolically ruler of their own "kingdom" meaning their lives, households, and the choices they make. But for now, here are a few key symbolic elements of a crown:

Authority and Power: A crown is often worn by a monarch or ruler to signify their legitimate authority and power over a nation or kingdom. It represents their right to govern and make decisions on behalf of their people. The crown is a visible reminder of the ruler's position at the top of the social and political hierarchy. In our case, each adult human being should have authority and power in their own lives.

Divinity and Sacredness: In many cultures, the crown is associated with divine right and represents a connection to the divine or spiritual realm. It symbolizes the ruler's divine mandate to govern and their role as a representative of the gods or a chosen deity. It reinforces the notion that the ruler is not just a mortal leader but possesses a special and elevated status. We believe every human being is made in the image and likeness of their Divine Creator.

Legitimacy and Succession: The crown is often passed down through generations, signifying the continuity and stability of a ruling dynasty. It represents the legitimacy of the ruler's claim to the throne and their rightful place in the succession line. The act of crowning a new monarch is a significant ritual that confirms their authority and marks the beginning of their reign. Each of us either as parents, guardians, aunts & uncles, mentors or simply role models should help to shape and mold the young princes and princesses who will become tomorrow's Kings and Queens.

Wealth and Status: Crowns are typically adorned with precious jewels such as gold, gemstones, and intricate designs. These elements symbolize the wealth, opulence, and extravagance associated with royalty. The crown serves as a visual display of the ruler's wealth and status, setting them apart from ordinary individuals and emphasizing their elevated position in society. Our "crowns" are symbolic, and while everyone may not become wealthy, we believe it is in everyone's ability to create a comfortable quality of life.

Achievement and Accomplishment: In addition to representing power and authority, a crown can also symbolize achievement and accomplishment. It is often bestowed as a reward or recognition for notable achievements, such as military victories or significant contributions to society. In this context, the crown serves as a symbol of honor and distinction. Likewise, our crowns represent knowledge and wisdom to create better "kingdoms" for ourselves and our families.

The Spiritual Crown Depicted as a Halo: A crown and a halo share a commonality in their symbolic representation of honor and distinction. Both are often associated with elevated status or divinity, although they differ in their cultural and religious contexts.

A crown, typically made of precious metals and adorned with jewels, is a regal headpiece worn by monarchs, royalty, or high-ranking individuals. It signifies authority, power, and sovereignty, often denoting the ruler's position or the achievements of the wearer. Crowns can vary in design and style, reflecting different historical periods and cultural traditions.

On the other hand, a halo is a luminous, circular aura depicted as a radiant ring of light around the head of a person, typically depicted in religious art. It is most associated with saints, angels, and divine beings across various faiths and belief systems. The halo represents holiness, spiritual enlightenment, and divine grace, symbolizing the individual's elevated and transcendent nature. Despite their distinct visual appearances and cultural associations, both the crown and the halo encapsulate the notion of honor, distinction, and elevated status. They serve as visual cues, conveying the exceptional qualities and elevated position of the wearer in their respective contexts. Our aim is for individuals to adorn a symbolic crown by becoming their best in body mind & spirit and taking ownership of their lives and ruling their worlds as their own kingdoms!

THE SYMBOLISM OF A JEWEL

Jewels have held symbolic significance throughout human history. They are prized for their beauty, rarity, and intrinsic value. While the primary symbolism of jewels typically revolves around beauty, wealth, and other aspects, the association of jewels with knowledge is less direct and yet in the hip-hop world sharing a "jewel" meant sharing some wisdom. For our "crowns," we believe each King or Queen needs seven essential "jewels" to build a "kingdom" or quality life for themselves. Before we describe our seven jewels for building Kings and Queens, we can explore a metaphorical interpretation in all that a jewel symbolizes. Here are some common symbolic meanings associated with jewels:

Beauty and Elegance: Jewels are often admired for their exquisite beauty, captivating colors, and sparkling brilliance. They represent aesthetics, grace, and elegance. Wearing or possessing jewels can enhance one's appearance and signify a sense of refinement and luxury. Each of us are divinely made and are unique in our own right.

Wealth and Status: Throughout history, jewels have been associated with wealth, prosperity, and social status. Owning and displaying jewels has been a symbol of affluence and power, highlighting one's ability to acquire rare and valuable possessions. Jewels have often been used to adorn crowns, tiaras, and other regal accessories, emphasizing the wearer's high rank and social standing. Your status comes from within and your outer lifestyle is a result of the energy, effort and consistency you've displayed over the years.

Protection and Amulet: Some cultures believe that certain gemstones possess protective properties and can ward off evil or negative energies. These gemstones are worn as amulets or talismans for personal safeguarding. For example, ancient civilizations believed that amethyst could protect against intoxication, while jade was considered to bring good fortune and protect against harm. In our case, your jewels of knowledge can serve as your protection from poor decisions and ignorance.

Love and Romance: Certain gemstones, such as diamonds, are strongly associated with love and romance. They are often used in engagement rings and wedding bands, symbolizing eternal love, commitment, and fidelity. Gemstones like rubies and garnets have also been linked to passion and desire. We value the importance of love, family and friends and thus this represents one of our jewels.

Spirituality and Enlightenment: Gemstones have been regarded as carriers of spiritual energy and have been used in various healing and spiritual practices. Different gemstones are believed to possess specific metaphysical properties and can be used to enhance spiritual well-being, balance energies, or promote personal growth and enlightenment. Part of our purpose in life is to grow and evolve. We should be better than the person we were yesterday. This "jewel" is spiritual growth.

Individuality and Personal Expression: The choice and wearing of specific jewels can reflect one's personal style, taste, and identity. Different gemstones are associated with birth months, zodiac signs, or personal characteristics. People often wear their birthstone to express their individuality and connect with their unique qualities. Each and every person's jewels attained will be unique and thus everyone's crown, meaning their life, will be unique.

Illumination and Awakening: Just as a jewel reflects and refracts light, knowledge illuminates the mind. Knowledge expands our understanding, helps us gain insights, and sheds light on previously unknown or misunderstood aspects of the world. In this sense, a jewel's brilliance can be seen as a metaphor for the enlightenment and clarity that knowledge brings. All attainments begin with exposure and knowledge.

Value and Rarity: Jewels are prized for their scarcity and value, and similarly, knowledge is highly valued for its scarcity in certain domains. Knowledge represents specialized expertise, wisdom, and intellectual depth. Like a rare gem, deep knowledge is something that not everyone possesses, making it highly sought after and esteemed. Your path and journey in life is unique as you are literally one out of billions.

Symbol of Wisdom: Throughout history and across cultures, jewels have been associated with wisdom and sagacity. This connection can be extended to knowledge, as knowledge is often seen as a source of wisdom. The pursuit of knowledge involves acquiring information, analyzing it critically, and using it to make informed decisions. Consequently, a jewel may symbolize the wisdom that comes from the accumulation and application of knowledge. True wisdom is attained only after many years of experience and mastery.

Transformation and Growth: Just as a rough gemstone is transformed into a polished jewel through cutting, shaping, and polishing, knowledge can transform an individual's understanding and perspective. The acquisition of knowledge leads to personal growth, intellectual development, and a broader worldview. In this sense, a jewel represents the transformative power of knowledge to refine and enhance one's abilities and outlook. This book will serve as your initial "tool." It is up to you to refine it and shape it to your personal liking and lifestyle.

WHAT IT MEANS TO BE A KING OR QUEEN

To be a king or queen metaphorically means embodying certain qualities and ideals that represent leadership, power, and influence. While traditionally associated with monarchy and royalty, being a king or queen in a metaphorical sense transcends titles and positions. It pertains to a state of mind, a set of values, and a way of conducting oneself in various aspects of life. Here, I'll delve into the metaphorical meaning of being a king or queen, encompassing key aspects such as character, responsibility, vision, and service.

Character: A true king or queen possesses exemplary character traits. They are known for their integrity, honesty, and moral uprightness. They lead by example, adhering to principles of fairness, compassion, and respect for others. They inspire trust and loyalty through their actions and words, and their character becomes the bedrock of their influence.

Responsibility: Kings and queens shoulder immense responsibility for the well-being of their kingdoms. Similarly, in a metaphorical sense, being a king or queen signifies embracing responsibility for one's own life, choices, and actions. It involves taking ownership of personal growth, cultivating self-discipline, and making wise decisions that impact not only oneself but also those around them such as family, friends and/or children.

Vision: A king or queen possesses a clear vision for their kingdom, envisioning a better future and charting a path to achieve it. Metaphorically, being a king or queen means having a vision for one's life, setting meaningful goals, and pursuing them with unwavering determination. It involves cultivating a sense of purpose and direction, continuously striving for self-improvement, and inspiring others to discover their own vision and purpose.

Leadership: Kings and queens are effective leaders who guide their kingdoms towards progress and prosperity. In a metaphorical context, being a king or queen implies exhibiting leadership qualities that inspire and motivate others. It involves the ability to communicate effectively, listen attentively, and empathize with others. True leaders encourage collaboration, foster a sense of unity, and empower those around them to reach their full potential.

Influence: A king or queen wields significant influence and has the power to make a positive impact on their kingdom. In a metaphorical sense, being a king or queen means recognizing the influence one holds in their personal and social spheres. It involves using that influence responsibly to uplift others, effect positive change, and advocate for justice and equality. A king or queen understands that their influence is not to be used for personal gain but to serve the greater good.

Wisdom: Kings and queens are known for their wisdom and sound judgment. Metaphorically, being a king or queen involves cultivating wisdom through knowledge, experience, and a willingness to learn from mistakes. It entails making well-informed decisions, seeking guidance from mentors, and continuously expanding one's intellectual and emotional intelligence.

Service: Lastly, a true king or queen serves their kingdom selflessly, prioritizing the well-being of their people above their own. In a metaphorical sense, being a king or queen means embracing a life of service to others. It involves compassionately assisting those in need, sharing knowledge and resources, and working towards creating a better world for all. True kings and queens understand that their leadership is not for personal glory, but to uplift and empower others.

In conclusion, to be a king or queen metaphorically goes beyond titles or positions. It represents embodying character, shouldering responsibility, having a vision, exhibiting leadership, wielding influence wisely, cultivating wisdom, and serving others. By embracing these qualities, one can strive to be a king or queen, creating a better "kingdom" in which to live and leaving a lasting positive impact on the world around them.

THE KINGDOM OF GOOD CHARACTER

Possessing good character is a fundamental aspect of personal growth and ethical behavior. It encompasses a set of positive qualities, values, and traits that guide our actions, choices, and interactions with others. Here, I will elaborate in greater detail on what it means to possess good character in building your kingdom:

Integrity: Good character involves having integrity, which means being honest, ethical, and consistent in your words and actions. It entails aligning your behavior with your values and principles, even when faced with difficult situations or temptations.

Honesty: Honest individuals uphold truthfulness and transparency in their interactions. They communicate truthfully, avoid deception or manipulation, and take responsibility for their actions. Honesty fosters trust, builds strong relationships, and promotes a sense of credibility and authenticity.

Trustworthiness: Trustworthiness is an essential component of good character. Trustworthy individuals keep their promises, honor commitments, and demonstrate reliability and dependability. They respect confidentiality and maintain the trust placed in them by others.

Respect: Possessing good character involves treating others with respect, regardless of their background, beliefs, or differences. Respectful individuals value the inherent worth and dignity of every person and show consideration for their feelings, opinions, and boundaries.

Responsibility: Good character entails taking responsibility for one's actions, decisions, and obligations. Responsible individuals understand the impact of their choices and accept the consequences that arise from them. They fulfill their commitments and contribute to their personal and social responsibilities.

Compassion: Compassion is a key aspect of good character. It involves showing empathy, kindness, and understanding toward others. Compassionate individuals are sensitive to the needs and struggles of others, and they extend support and assistance when possible.

Fairness & Justice: Good character encompasses a commitment to fairness and justice. Fair individuals treat others impartially, without favoritism or discrimination. They uphold principles of equality, equity, and fairness in their interactions and decision-making processes.

Humility: Possessing good character includes humility, which involves recognizing and acknowledging one's strengths and weaknesses. Humble individuals are open to learning, receptive to feedback, and modest about their achievements. They value others' perspectives and embrace opportunities for personal growth.

Courage: Good character encompasses courage, the ability to face challenges, adversity, and difficult situations with bravery and resilience. Courageous individuals demonstrate morai courage by standing up for what is right, even in the face of opposition or risk.

Generosity: Good character involves being generous and giving of oneself. Generous individuals share their time, resources, and talents to help others without expecting anything in return. They understand the importance of contributing to the well-being of their communities and making a positive impact in the world.

Gratitude: Good character includes cultivating a sense of gratitude and appreciation for the blessings and opportunities in life. Grateful individuals recognize and express gratitude for the kindness and support they receive from others, fostering a positive and appreciative outlook.

Self-Discipline: Possessing good character requires self-discipline. Self-disciplined individuals exhibit self-control, manage their impulses, and follow through on their commitments. They prioritize long-term goals over short-term gratification and demonstrate perseverance in pursuing their aspirations.

Empathy: Good character involves empathy, the ability to understand and share the feelings and experiences of others. Empathetic individuals listen attentively, show compassion, and strive to support others emotionally and mentally.

Open-Mindedness: Good character encompasses open-mindedness, being receptive to different perspectives, ideas, and beliefs. Open-minded individuals are willing to consider alternative viewpoints, engage in constructive dialogue, and embrace diversity.

Continuous Improvement: Possessing good character entails a commitment to continuous self-improvement. People of good character practice self-reflection, evaluation, and objectivity. They recognize that there is always room for growth and improvement no matter what their status in life may be.

THE KINGDOM OF RESPONSIBILITY

Personal Responsibility: Practicing personal responsibility means recognizing that you are in control of your own life and the outcomes of your choices. It involves taking ownership of your thoughts, emotions, actions, and decisions. You understand that you have the power to shape your circumstances and take proactive steps to create positive change. Regardless of where you were born, where you begin in life, the shorthand you may have been dealt or the environment you are in, making the right choices in life can change your tomorrow. We acknowledge some situations may be more difficult than others, but chances are no matter where you are in life, there is someone out there dealing with worse circumstances. Thus, accept your status and work tirelessly to improve it.

Fulfilling Commitments: Being responsible entails fulfilling the commitments and obligations you make to yourself and others. Whether it's meeting deadlines at work, honoring agreements with friends, or keeping promises to yourself, responsible individuals prioritize their commitments and take them seriously. They understand the importance of trust and reliability in maintaining healthy relationships and achieving personal and professional success.

Reliability and Dependability: Responsible individuals are reliable and dependable. They can be counted on to follow through on their commitments, meet deadlines, and deliver on their promises. They understand the value of being consistent and trustworthy, and they strive to maintain their reputation for reliability.

Taking Initiative: Practicing responsibility involves taking initiative and being proactive in addressing challenges and opportunities. Responsible individuals don't wait for others to take action or for circumstances to change; they take the lead and initiate necessary steps to achieve their goals. They are self-motivated, resourceful, and willing to put in the effort required to accomplish their objectives.

Admitting Mistakes: Accountability is an integral part of responsibility. Responsible individuals acknowledge and take responsibility for their mistakes and shortcomings. They don't shy away from admitting when they are wrong or have made an error. Instead, they learn from their mistakes, make amends if necessary, and take steps to prevent similar errors in the future.

Problem-Solving: Responsible individuals are proactive problem-solvers. Instead of blaming others or external circumstances, they focus on finding solutions to challenges and obstacles. They analyze situations objectively, identify possible alternatives, and take decisive actions to address problems effectively.

Ethical Decision-Making: Practicing responsibility involves making ethical decisions and considering the impact of your choices on others and the broader community. Responsible individuals strive to act in accordance with moral principles and values, even when it may be difficult or inconvenient. They consider the consequences of their actions and make choices that align with their ethical compass.

Time Management: Responsible individuals understand the importance of managing their time effectively. They prioritize tasks, set realistic deadlines, and allocate their time efficiently. They avoid procrastination and strive to meet their obligations within the given time frames.

Professionalism: Responsibility is integral to professionalism in the business or the workplace. Responsible individuals and leaders demonstrate professionalism by being punctual, meeting work expectations, and honoring professional standards. They take pride in their work and contribute to a positive and productive work environment.

Accepting Feedback: Responsible individuals are open to feedback and constructive criticism. They view feedback as an opportunity for growth and improvement. They listen attentively, reflect on the feedback received, and take necessary actions to enhance their performance and skills.

Environmental Responsibility: Responsibility extends beyond personal actions to include environmental consciousness. Responsible individuals recognize the importance of sustainability and take steps to minimize their environmental impact. They practice recycling, conserve energy and water, and make environmentally conscious choices in their daily lives.

Community Engagement: Practicing responsibility involves actively participating in and contributing to your community. Responsible individuals understand their role as citizens and engage in volunteer work, community initiatives, or other forms of service. They recognize the importance of giving back and making a positive impact on the lives of others.

THE KINGDOM OF VISION

Being visionary refers to possessing a forward-thinking mindset and the ability to envision and pursue a compelling future. Visionary individuals have a clear sense of purpose, can see possibilities beyond the current reality, and inspire others to join them in their pursuit. Here, I will elaborate in greater detail on what it means to be visionary in building your kingdom:

Clarity of Purpose: Visionary individuals have a deep understanding of their purpose and mission. They have a clear vision of what they want to achieve and why it matters. This clarity serves as a guiding light that shapes their decisions, actions, and priorities.

Big Picture Thinking: Visionaries possess the ability to see the big picture. They have a broader perspective beyond immediate challenges or short-term goals. They understand how different elements connect and impact each other, enabling them to anticipate trends, patterns, and potential outcomes.

Future Orientation: Visionaries are future-oriented. They focus on possibilities and are not bound by present limitations. They imagine a better future and work towards creating it, even when it seems distant or unattainable. Their mindset allows them to think beyond the status quo and envision innovative solutions.

Innovation and Creativity: Being visionary involves fostering a spirit of innovation and creativity. Visionaries are not afraid to challenge conventional wisdom and think outside the box. They seek novel approaches, embrace change, and are willing to take calculated risks to bring their ideas to life.

Inspiring and Influencing Others: Visionary individuals can inspire and influence others with their compelling vision. They possess strong communication skills and effectively articulate their ideas, generating enthusiasm and motivation among those around them. They inspire individuals to believe in the vision and actively contribute to its realization.

Strategic Planning: Visionaries are adept at strategic planning. They can break down their vision into actionable steps and develop long-term plans to achieve their goals. They possess the ability to anticipate obstacles and devise contingency plans to overcome them. Their strategic approach ensures that their vision is translated into practical actions.

Resilience and Persistence: Being visionary requires resilience and persistence. Visionaries encounter setbacks, face resistance, and encounter obstacles along the way. However, their unwavering belief in their vision and determination to make it a reality allow them to persevere through challenges and setbacks.

Embracing Change: Visionaries embrace change and see it as an opportunity for growth and improvement. They recognize that change is inevitable and adapt their plans and strategies accordingly. They are flexible and open to new ideas, technologies, and trends that can further enhance their vision.

Collaboration and Team Building: Visionaries understand the power of collaboration and team building. They bring together individuals who share their passion and complement their skills to collectively work towards the shared vision. They foster an inclusive and supportive environment that encourages collaboration, creativity, and collective ownership.

Impact and Legacy: Visionaries aspire to make a significant impact and leave a lasting legacy. They strive to create positive change that transcends their individual contributions. They consider the long-term consequences of their actions and work towards creating a legacy that inspires future generations.

Lifelong Learning: Being visionary involves a commitment to lifelong learning and personal development. Visionaries continuously seek knowledge, explore new ideas, and stay abreast of emerging trends and technologies. They invest in their own growth to expand their perspective and adapt their vision to evolving circumstances.

Empathy and Social Responsibility: Visionary individuals possess empathy and a sense of social responsibility. They consider the needs and aspirations of others and strive to create a positive impact on society. They leverage their vision to address societal challenges, promote equality, and uplift the lives of others.

THE KINGDOM OF LEADERSHIP

Being a good leader entails possessing a range of qualities, skills, and behaviors that inspire and guide others toward a common goal. Good leaders not only achieve results but also foster a positive and supportive environment that promotes growth and development. Here, I will elaborate in greater detail on what it means to be a good leader in building your kingdom:

Vision and Purpose: A good leader has a clear vision and purpose. They articulate a compelling vision that inspires and motivates others. They communicate the mission effectively, ensuring that everyone understands the direction and goals of the team or organization.

Integrity and Trustworthiness: Good leaders demonstrate integrity and are trusted by their team members. They act ethically, consistently aligning their actions with their words and values. They build trust through honesty, transparency, and reliability, fostering an environment of trust and respect.

Effective Communication: Good leaders excel in communication. They listen actively and empathetically, seeking to understand others' perspectives. They express their ideas clearly and concisely, fostering open and transparent communication within the team. They provide constructive feedback and encourage dialogue, promoting a culture of collaboration.

Emotional Intelligence: Good leaders possess emotional intelligence, which includes self-awareness, empathy, and effective interpersonal skills. They understand their own emotions and manage them in a constructive manner. They also understand and empathize with the emotions of others, building strong relationships and fostering a positive team dynamic.

Decisiveness: Good leaders are decisive and capable of making timely and informed decisions. They gather relevant information, analyze options, and consider the potential impact on the team or organization. They weigh risks and benefits, and once a decision is made, they take responsibility for its implementation.

Strategic Thinking: Good leaders have strong strategic thinking abilities. They see the big picture, anticipate future trends and challenges, and make decisions that align with long-term goals. They analyze complex situations, identify opportunities, and develop effective strategies to achieve desired outcomes.

Empowerment and Delegation: Good leaders empower and delegate tasks effectively. They trust their team members, provide them with autonomy and authority, and delegate responsibilities according to individual strengths and capabilities. They foster a culture of empowerment, enabling team members to grow, take ownership, and contribute their best.

Coaching and Mentoring: Good leaders are effective coaches and mentors. They support the development of their team members by providing guidance, feedback, and opportunities for growth. They recognize and cultivate individual strengths, identify areas for improvement, and invest in their team's professional development.

Resilience and Adaptability: Good leaders demonstrate resilience and adaptability in the face of challenges and change. They remain calm under pressure, navigate uncertainties, and inspire confidence in their team. They are flexible and open to new ideas, willing to adapt strategies as needed to achieve desired outcomes.

Collaboration and Team Building: Good leaders foster collaboration and create a cohesive team environment. They encourage diversity of thought, promote effective teamwork, and build strong relationships based on trust and respect. They harness the collective talents and strengths of their team members to achieve shared goals.

Accountability: Good leaders hold themselves and others accountable. They take responsibility for their actions, admit mistakes, and learn from failures. They establish clear expectations, set measurable goals, and ensure that individuals are accountable for their performance and contributions.

Continuous Learning: Good leaders are lifelong learners. They seek opportunities to expand their knowledge, develop new skills, and stay updated with industry trends. They encourage a culture of continuous learning within their team, fostering innovation, adaptability, and personal growth.

Empathy and Inclusivity: Good leaders demonstrate empathy and inclusivity. They consider the needs and perspectives of diverse individuals and create an inclusive environment where everyone feels valued and heard. They champion diversity and foster a sense.

THE KINGDOM OF INFLUENCE

Being an influencer refers to having the ability to impact and shape the thoughts, behaviors, and actions of others. Influencers can possess a significant following or reach online, or just at home or in their community, and they leverage their "platforms" to inspire, educate, entertain, or create positive change on a small or large scale. Here, I will elaborate in greater detail on what it means to be an influencer in building your kingdom:

Authenticity: Authenticity is a key aspect of being an influencer. Influencers are true to themselves and their values, and they express their genuine opinions and beliefs. They build trust with their audience by being transparent, honest, and relatable.

Expertise and Knowledge: Influencers have expertise or knowledge in a particular field, niche, or subject matter. They establish themselves as credible sources of information and provide valuable insights, tips, and advice to their audience. They continuously invest in their knowledge and stay updated with the latest trends and developments.

Engaging Content Creation: Influencers create engaging and compelling content that resonates with their audience. They use various media formats, such as videos, blogs, podcasts, or social media posts, to deliver their message effectively. They understand their audience's preferences and tailor their content to cater to their interests and needs.

Building a Community: Influencers focus on building a community around their content. They foster meaningful connections with their followers, encourage interaction and engagement, and create a sense of belonging. They respond to comments, messages, and feedback, fostering a two-way communication channel.

Positive Influence and Impact: Influencers strive to have a positive influence and impact on their audience. They inspire, motivate, educate, or entertain their followers, aiming to make a difference in their lives. They use their platform responsibly to promote positive values, behaviors, and social causes.

Collaboration and Partnerships: Influencers often collaborate with brands, other influencers, or organizations that align with their values and audience. They engage in partnerships to create mutually beneficial content, promote products or services, or support causes they believe in. They approach collaborations with authenticity and transparency.

Adaptability and Relevance: Influencers understand the importance of staying adaptable and relevant in a rapidly changing digital landscape. They embrace new platforms, trends, and technologies, and adjust their content strategy accordingly. They keep up with the evolving needs and preferences of their audience.

Ethics and Transparency: Influencers uphold ethical standards and transparency in their interactions with their audience and brand partnerships. They disclose sponsored or paid collaborations, clearly differentiate between opinions and endorsements, and maintain transparency in their content creation process.

Responsiveness and Engagement: Influencers actively engage with their audience and demonstrate responsiveness. They value the feedback and input of their followers, and they participate in conversations, answer questions, and address concerns. They create a sense of community by fostering a genuine connection with their audience.

Personal Branding: Influencers cultivate a strong personal brand. They develop a distinct identity, voice, and style that sets them apart from others. They consistently communicate their values, interests, and expertise, establishing a recognizable and authentic personal brand.

Continuous Growth and Learning: Influencers recognize the importance of continuous growth and learning. They seek opportunities to expand their knowledge, refine their skills, and adapt to industry changes. They actively engage with their audience's feedback and iterate their content strategy to improve and provide more value.

Social Responsibility: Influencers understand their role as public figures and the impact they can have on society. They use their influence to raise awareness about social issues, promote inclusivity and diversity, and support meaningful causes. They leverage their platform for positive change and strive to make a difference beyond their personal success. Being an influencer requires dedication, consistency, and a genuine passion for creating meaningful connections and making a positive impact on others.

THE KINGDOM OF WISDOM

Gaining wisdom is a lifelong journey of acquiring knowledge, experience, and insights that enable individuals to make wise decisions, navigate challenges, and live a more fulfilling life. Wisdom goes beyond mere knowledge and encompasses a deeper understanding of oneself, others, and the world. Here, I will elaborate in greater detail on what it means to gain wisdom in building your kingdom:

Self-Reflection and Awareness: Gaining wisdom begins with self-reflection and self-awareness. It involves understanding one's strengths, weaknesses, values, beliefs, and motivations. Self-reflection allows individuals to gain insight into their thoughts, emotions, and behaviors, leading to personal growth and self-improvement.

Seeking Knowledge: Wisdom is rooted in knowledge. Gaining wisdom requires a thirst for learning and a commitment to acquiring knowledge from various sources. It involves reading books, seeking mentorship, attending seminars, engaging in meaningful conversations, and exploring different perspectives to broaden one's understanding of the world.

Critical Thinking: Wisdom involves developing strong critical thinking skills. It requires the ability to analyze information, evaluate evidence, and think rationally and objectively. Critical thinking helps individuals make informed decisions, solve problems, and navigate complex situations with clarity and sound judgment.

Experience and Reflection: Wisdom is often gained through firsthand experience and reflection. It involves learning from both successes and failures, and extracting valuable lessons from past experiences. Reflecting on experiences allows individuals to gain deeper insights, identify patterns, and make better choices in the future.

Emotional Intelligence: Wisdom encompasses emotional intelligence, which involves understanding and managing one's emotions and empathizing with others. Emotional intelligence enables individuals to navigate relationships, resolve conflicts, and make decisions with empathy and compassion. It fosters better understanding of oneself and others, leading to more meaningful connections.

Open-Mindedness: Gaining wisdom requires open-mindedness and a willingness to consider different perspectives and ideas. It involves challenging one's own beliefs and biases, being receptive to new information, and embracing diverse viewpoints. Open-mindedness allows individuals to expand their understanding and grow intellectually and emotionally.

Humility: Wisdom is closely tied to humility. It involves recognizing the limits of one's knowledge and being open to continuous learning and growth. Humility allows individuals to seek advice, acknowledge mistakes, and learn from others. It fosters a sense of curiosity and a willingness to embrace new insights and ideas.

Decision-Making: Wisdom is reflected in the ability to make sound decisions. It involves considering long-term consequences, weighing different options, and aligning decisions with one's values and principles. Wise decision-making takes into account the perspectives of others and aims to achieve the greatest good for oneself and others.

Ethics and Morality: Wisdom is intertwined with ethics and morality. It involves making choices that align with ethical principles and moral values. Wise individuals consider the impact of their actions on others and strive to act in a way that promotes fairness, justice, and integrity.

Applying Knowledge: Wisdom is not solely about knowledge acquisition but also about applying that knowledge effectively in real-life situations. Wise individuals use their knowledge and insights to solve problems, make ethical choices, and contribute positively to their communities. They translate their understanding into practical actions that create meaningful impact.

Mentorship and Guidance: Gaining wisdom can be facilitated through mentorship and guidance from wise individuals. Mentors provide valuable guidance, share their experiences and insights, and offer support in the pursuit of wisdom. Learning from those who have already gained wisdom can accelerate one's own journey.

Continuous Growth and Reflection: Gaining wisdom is an ongoing process. It requires a commitment to continuous growth, learning, and self-reflection. Wise individuals regularly assess their beliefs, actions, and perspectives, seeking opportunities for improvement and personal development.

THE KINGDOM OF SERVICE

Providing service to others is an act of selflessness and a commitment to contributing to the well-being and betterment of individuals, communities, or society as a whole. It involves using one's skills, resources, and time to make a positive impact and improve the lives of others. Here, I will elaborate in greater detail on what it means to provide service to others in building your kingdom:

Altruism and Empathy: Service to others is rooted in altruism and empathy. It involves genuinely caring about the welfare and needs of others, putting their interests before one's own, and seeking to alleviate their suffering or improve their circumstances. Empathy allows individuals to understand and relate to the experiences and emotions of others, fostering a sense of compassion and connection.

Identifying Needs: Providing service requires identifying the needs of others. It involves actively listening, observing, and engaging with individuals or communities to understand their challenges, struggles, and aspirations. By recognizing specific needs, it becomes possible to offer meaningful assistance and support.

Volunteerism: Service often involves volunteering one's time, skills, or expertise. It may include working with nonprofit organizations, community groups, or charitable initiatives. Volunteering allows individuals to directly engage in activities that address social issues, support causes they believe in, and make a tangible difference in the lives of others.

Sharing Knowledge and Skills: Service can involve sharing knowledge, skills, or expertise to empower others. It may include teaching, mentoring, or providing guidance in areas where one has expertise. By imparting knowledge and skills, individuals can help others develop their capabilities, gain confidence, and achieve their goals.

Philanthropy and Charitable Giving: Service can also involve philanthropy and charitable giving. It may include donating resources, such as money, goods, or services, to organizations or individuals in need. Philanthropic efforts can support education, healthcare, poverty alleviation, environmental conservation, or other social causes.

Advocacy and Activism: Service can take the form of advocacy and activism. It involves raising awareness about social issues, speaking up for marginalized or disadvantaged groups, and advocating for policy changes or societal improvements. By using one's voice and influence, individuals can create awareness, mobilize support, and drive positive change.

Supporting Personal Development: Service to others can also involve supporting the personal development and growth of individuals. It may include mentoring, coaching, or providing guidance to help others unlock their potential, overcome obstacles, and achieve personal or professional goals. By investing in the growth of others, individuals can empower them to lead fulfilling and meaningful lives.

Building Relationships and Connections: Service often involves building meaningful relationships and connections with others. It includes fostering a sense of community, creating a supportive network, and forging connections based on trust, respect, and mutual understanding. Building relationships allows individuals to provide emotional support, create a sense of belonging, and contribute to the social fabric of communities.

Engaging in Random Acts of Kindness: Service can be as simple as engaging in random acts of kindness. It involves performing small acts of generosity, compassion, or assistance without expecting anything in return. Random acts of kindness have the power to brighten someone's day, inspire others, and create a ripple effect of positivity.

Sustainability and Long-Term Impact: Service to others involves considering the long-term impact of one's actions. It entails addressing root causes of problems, promoting sustainable solutions, and working towards systemic change. By focusing on long-term impact, individuals can create lasting improvements and contribute to the overall well-being of communities or society.

Cultivating a Service Mindset: Providing service requires cultivating a service mindset. It involves embracing the values of humility, gratitude, and a genuine desire to contribute to the greater good. Cultivating a service mindset involves adopting a perspective and approach to life that prioritizes helping and serving others. It goes beyond personal interests and focuses on making a positive impact on individuals, communities, or even the world at large. A service mindset encompasses empathy, compassion, and a genuine desire to contribute to the well-being of others.

THE SEVEN JEWELS FOR BUILDING KINGS & QUEENS

The seven jewels of financial wellness, asset ownership, strategic education, healthy living, family, spiritual growth, and paying it forward, are integral aspects of a well-rounded and fulfilled life and conducting one's self as a King or Queen. Each jewel contributes to an individual's overall well-being, both financially and emotionally. Let's delve into the importance of each of these jewels:

THE 1ST JEWEL: Financial Wellness: Financial wellness refers to the state of one's overall financial health and stability. It encompasses various aspects such as managing income, expenses, debt, savings, and investments. Achieving financial wellness is crucial because it provides a foundation for a secure and fulfilling life. It reduces financial stress, promotes peace of mind, and allows individuals to pursue their goals and aspirations. Financial wellness enables people to effectively plan for the future, build wealth, and overcome financial challenges, ultimately leading to greater freedom and opportunities.

THE 2ND JEWEL: Asset Ownership: Asset ownership involves accumulating and managing tangible and intangible assets such as real estate, investments, business ventures, intellectual property, and more. Owning assets is important as it provides a means to generate income, grow wealth, and create a sense of security. Assets generally appreciate over time and thus can serve as a safety net during emergencies or retirement. They also offer opportunities for diversification and can be passed on to future generations, facilitating inter-generational wealth transfer.

THE 3RD JEWEL: Strategic Education: Strategic education emphasizes the acquisition of knowledge and skills necessary for making informed life choices. It includes gaining the essential life skills, knowledge, talents and abilities in the most effective manner possible. Strategic education is important because it empowers individuals to take control of their lives and better control its direction. It enables them to navigate challenging situations, recognize and seize opportunities, and protect themselves from changing times. By continually learning and staying informed, individuals can adapt to changing economic landscapes, obtain good careers, create profitable businesses, enhance their earning potential, and make sound financial choices.

THE 4TH JEWEL: Healthy Living: Healthy living encompasses physical, mental, and emotional well-being. It involves adopting habits and practices that promote good physical health, such as regular exercise, a balanced diet, and sufficient rest. Additionally, maintaining positive mental and emotional health through stress management, self-care, and seeking support from experts when needed is crucial. Healthy living is vital because it directly impacts an individual's quality of life and financial well-being. It reduces healthcare costs, increases productivity, and enhances the ability to earn income. By prioritizing health, individuals can improve their overall financial resilience, live longer and enjoy a more fulfilling life.

THE 5TH JEWEL: Family: Family is an essential cornerstone of our lives, providing emotional support, love, and a nurturing environment. The bonds we form within our families shape our identity, influence our values, and provide a lifelong network of support. Recognizing the importance of family and nurturing those relationships can contribute to our overall well-being and happiness. Work-life balance refers to maintaining a harmonious equilibrium between work responsibilities and personal life commitments. Striking a balance is important because it helps prevent burnout, improves mental health, and enhances overall well-being. When one can allocate time and energy to their personal lives, relationships, hobbies, and self-care, they experience greater life satisfaction.

THE 6TH JEWEL: Spiritual Growth: Spiritual growth involves exploring and nurturing one's sense of purpose, meaning, and connection to something greater than oneself. It can be pursued through various practices, including meditation, self-reflection, and engaging in activities aligned with personal values. Spiritual growth is important as it cultivates inner peace, resilience, and a deeper understanding of oneself and the world. It provides a sense of fulfillment beyond material possessions, reducing the reliance on consumerism and external validation. By focusing on spiritual growth, individuals can align their financial choices with their core values, make meaningful contributions to society, and find contentment.

THE 7ᵀᴴ JEWEL: Paying It Forward: Paying it forward refers to acts of generosity, kindness, and contributing to the well-being of others without expecting anything in return. Engaging in philanthropy, volunteering, or supporting charitable causes promotes empathy, compassion, and social responsibility. Paying it forward is important as it creates a positive ripple effect in society. It strengthens communities, addresses social issues, and fosters a sense of collective well-being. Additionally, acts of giving and helping others have been shown.

In conclusion, each of the seven jewels play a vital role in achieving overall well-being, happiness, and long-term financial success. By focusing on financial smarts, asset ownership, strategic education, healthy living, family & friends, spiritual growth, and paying it forward, individuals can cultivate a fulfilling and prosperous life, where financial stability and personal well-being are intertwined. It is important to recognize that these jewels are interconnected and should be approached holistically to maximize their impact and create a life of abundance and purpose.

THE 1ST JEWEL:
FINANCIAL WELLNESS

The current state of the world does not allow for everyone to be wealthy. Despite this fact, it is still possible for someone to not simply be a slave to work. With proper financial knowledge, many of us can attain a good quality of life and enjoy a lifestyle that is satisfying and fulfilling. It is very difficult for someone living in poverty or from paycheck to paycheck to have the time to develop other areas of their life. Hence it is imperative for individuals to learn as early as possible how to make money, manage finances and hopefully share this knowledge with friends and offspring so they get a head start.

Financial wellness refers to the state of one's overall financial health and well-being. It encompasses various aspects of personal finance, including income, expenses, savings, investments, debt management, and long-term financial planning. Achieving financial wellness involves adopting positive financial habits, making informed decisions, and maintaining a sense of control and security over one's financial circumstances. Here, I will provide a thorough and detailed explanation of the key components of financial wellness towards building a stable kingdom:

Budgeting and Spending: A crucial aspect of financial wellness is budgeting. It involves creating a detailed plan for income allocation, ensuring that expenses align with income levels and financial goals. Effective budgeting helps individuals prioritize their spending, track their expenses, and make informed choices about where their money goes. It allows for responsible spending, reducing the risk of overspending and financial stress.

Income and Savings: Financial wellness involves having a stable and sustainable income source. This can be through employment, self-employment, business ownership, royalties, investments, or a combination of various income streams. Adequate income helps cover expenses, build savings, and prepare for unexpected financial challenges. Additionally, maintaining a habit of regular saving is crucial for financial wellness. Setting aside a portion of income for emergencies, future goals, and retirement ensures long-term financial security.

Debt Management: Effectively managing debt is a significant component of financial wellness. It involves understanding and monitoring existing debts, such as credit card debt, student loans, or mortgages. Developing a strategy to pay off debt, prioritizing high-interest debt, and making consistent payments helps reduce financial burdens and improves overall financial well-being.

Financial Planning: Financial wellness necessitates having a long-term financial plan. This includes setting financial goals, such as buying a house, funding education, starting a business, or retiring comfortably. A comprehensive financial plan considers income, expenses, savings, investments, insurance, and retirement planning. It helps individuals make informed decisions, allocate resources effectively, and work towards achieving their financial objectives.

Risk Management and Insurance: Mitigating financial risks is an essential aspect of financial wellness. This involves obtaining appropriate insurance coverage, such as health insurance, life insurance, disability insurance, and property insurance. Insurance provides protection against unexpected events, reduces financial vulnerability, and ensures financial stability during challenging times.

Investment and Wealth Building: Building wealth and growing financial assets is a vital part of financial wellness. It involves understanding investment options, such as stocks, bonds, real estate, and retirement accounts. Making informed investment decisions based on risk tolerance, financial goals, and market conditions helps individuals grow their wealth over time and secure their financial future.

Financial Education and Awareness: Enhancing financial literacy and staying informed about personal finance concepts is crucial for financial wellness. Continuous learning and understanding of financial concepts, such as budgeting, investing, and managing credit, empower individuals to make informed decisions and navigate complex financial landscapes effectively.

Achieving financial wellness is an ongoing process that requires discipline, knowledge, and proactive decision-making. By adopting positive financial habits, setting goals, and taking control of their financial circumstances, individuals can improve their overall well-being and achieve long-term financial security. Financial wellness provides a foundation for personal growth, reduces stress, and enables individuals to make choices that align with their values and aspirations.

THE KINGDOM OF BUDGETING & SPENDING

Effective budgeting and spending are crucial components of financial wellness. They involve creating a detailed plan for income allocation, managing expenses, and making informed choices about how money is spent. Let's delve into greater detail about what effective budgeting and spending entail:

Creating a Budget: The first step in effective budgeting is creating a comprehensive budget. Start by gathering information about your income sources, such as salaries, bonuses, freelance work, or investment returns. Next, list all your expenses, including fixed costs like rent/mortgage, utilities, transportation, and variable expenses like groceries, dining out, entertainment, and discretionary spending. It's important to account for all expenses, both essential and non-essential.

Categorizing Expenses: Once you have a list of expenses, categorize them into different categories such as housing, transportation, groceries, utilities, debt payments, entertainment, and savings. This categorization helps you gain a clear understanding of where your money is going and identify areas where you may need to make adjustments.

Setting Financial Goals: Effective budgeting involves setting financial goals that align with your priorities. These goals could include saving for emergencies, paying off debts, saving for retirement, buying a house, or funding education. Having specific goals helps you prioritize your spending and make informed choices about where to allocate your financial resources.

Tracking Income and Expenses: To effectively manage your budget, it's important to track your income and expenses regularly. This can be done manually using spreadsheets or through budgeting apps and software. By monitoring your income and expenses, you gain insights into your spending patterns and can make adjustments as needed.

Differentiating Between Needs and Wants: A key aspect of effective budgeting and spending is distinguishing between needs and wants. Essential needs like housing, food, utilities, and healthcare should be prioritized, while discretionary expenses like dining out or entertainment can be adjusted based on your financial goals and priorities.

Prioritizing Saving: Effective budgeting involves prioritizing saving and allocating a portion of your income towards building an emergency fund and long-term savings. Saving is crucial for financial security and achieving your financial goals. Aim to save a percentage of your income each month and automate the process by setting up automatic transfers to your savings account.

Analyzing and Adjusting: Regularly reviewing your budget and analyzing your spending patterns is essential. This allows you to identify areas where you may be overspending or areas where you can potentially save more. Adjustments can be made by reducing expenses in certain categories, negotiating bills or subscriptions, or finding ways to increase your income.

Managing Debt: When budgeting, it's important to consider debt payments. Allocate a portion of your income towards paying off debts, such as credit card debt, student loans, or mortgages. Prioritize higher-interest debts to minimize interest payments and work towards becoming debt-free.

Flexibility and Adaptability: Life circumstances may change, and unexpected expenses may arise. Effective budgeting involves flexibility and adaptability to accommodate these changes. Be prepared to adjust your budget when necessary and make informed choices to maintain financial stability.

Seeking Professional Advice: If needed, consider seeking advice from financial professionals, such as financial advisors or credit counselors. They can provide guidance on budgeting techniques, debt management strategies, and help you optimize your financial decisions. Remember, effective budgeting and spending are ongoing processes. Regularly reviewing and adjusting your budget based on your financial goals and priorities is essential for maintaining financial wellness. By being intentional with your spending, making informed choices, and living within your means, you can achieve financial security and work towards your long-term financial aspirations.

THE KINGDOM OF INCOME & SAVINGS

Creating income and building savings are important aspects of financial wellness. Let's explore in greater detail how you can effectively create income and develop a habit of saving:

CREATING INCOME
Enhancing Employability: Invest in developing your skills and knowledge to increase your employability. Take courses, attend workshops, or pursue certifications to expand your expertise and make yourself more valuable in the job market.

Career Advancement: Seek opportunities for career advancement within your current organization or explore new job prospects that offer higher income potential. Continuously strive to improve your performance, take on additional responsibilities, and demonstrate your value to employers.

Side Hustles and Freelancing: Consider taking on side hustles or freelance work to supplement your primary income. Identify your skills and talents that can be monetized, such as graphic design, writing, tutoring, or consulting. Utilize online platforms and marketplaces to find clients and generate additional income.

Passive Income Streams: Explore passive income opportunities, such as investing in stocks, real estate, or creating digital products like e-books or online courses. These endeavors have the potential to generate ongoing income with minimal effort once established.

DEVELOPING A SAVINGS HABIT
Set Savings Goals: Define your savings goals based on short-term and long-term objectives. Whether it's building an emergency fund, saving for a down payment on a house, or planning for retirement, having specific goals helps motivate you to save.

Track Expenses: Keep track of your expenses to understand your spending patterns and identify areas where you can cut back or save more. Use budgeting apps or spreadsheets to monitor your financial transactions and categorize your expenses.

Automate Savings: Set up automatic transfers from your income to your savings account. By automating your savings, a predetermined portion of your income will be set aside without any effort or temptation to spend it.

Start Small and Increase Savings: If saving seems challenging, start with a small percentage of your income, and gradually increase it over time. Every contribution counts, and as you witness your savings grow, it can motivate you to save more.

Reduce Expenses: Review your expenses regularly and identify areas where you can reduce costs. Cut back on non-essential expenses, negotiate bills or subscriptions for better deals, and find ways to save on everyday expenses.

Avoid Impulse Purchases: Practice mindful spending and avoid impulse purchases. Before making a purchase, evaluate whether it aligns with your financial goals and if it truly adds value to your life. Delaying gratification can help you make more intentional spending choices.

Create a Budget: As mentioned before, creating and following a budget is crucial. Allocate a portion of your income explicitly towards savings and treat it as an essential expense. Make saving a priority rather than an afterthought.

Emergency Fund: Building an emergency fund is essential to protect yourself from unexpected financial setbacks. Aim to save at least three to six months' worth of living expenses to provide a safety net in case of job loss, medical emergencies, or other unforeseen circumstances.

Review and Adjust: Regularly review your savings progress and adjust your savings plan as needed. Celebrate milestones, reassess your goals, and make necessary modifications to stay on track.

Seek Professional Advice: If you need guidance, consider consulting with a financial advisor who can provide personalized recommendations based on your financial situation and goals. They can offer insights on investment options, retirement planning, and help optimize your savings strategy. Remember, building savings and creating income require patience, discipline, and consistent effort. By setting goals, being intentional with your income, and developing a habit of saving, you can make significant progress toward achieving financial stability and long-term financial success.

DEBT MANAGEMENT

Managing debt involves effectively handling and controlling the debts you owe to lenders or financial institutions. It entails making responsible decisions, organizing your finances, and implementing strategies to repay your debts while maintaining your overall financial health. Here, I will elaborate in greater detail on what it means to manage debt in building your kingdom:

Assessing Your Debt: To effectively manage debt, start by assessing your overall debt situation. List down all your debts, including credit card balances, loans, mortgages, or any other financial obligations. Take note of the outstanding amounts, interest rates, and payment terms associated with each debt.

Creating a Budget: Developing a budget is crucial for managing debt. Create a comprehensive budget that outlines your income, expenses, and debt obligations. Allocate funds specifically for debt repayments, ensuring that you have a realistic and sustainable plan for meeting your financial obligations.

Prioritizing Debt Repayment: Prioritize your debts based on factors such as interest rates, minimum payments, and outstanding balances. Consider implementing either the debt avalanche method (paying off high-interest debts first) or the debt snowball method (paying off smaller debts first for motivational purposes). Devote as much of your available funds as possible towards repaying high-interest debts while making minimum payments on other debts.

Negotiating with Creditors: If you're struggling to meet your debt obligations, consider negotiating with your creditors. Contact them to discuss potential options such as interest rate reductions, extended payment terms, or debt consolidation. Many creditors are willing to work with you to find a mutually beneficial solution that allows you to repay your debts.

Controlling Spending: Managing debt often requires controlling your spending habits. Analyze your expenses and identify areas where you can cut back or adjust. Limit unnecessary purchases, reduce discretionary spending, and focus on essential needs. Use your budget as a guide to ensure you allocate enough funds towards debt repayment.

Building an Emergency Fund: Establishing an emergency fund is essential for managing debt effectively. Set aside a portion of your income to create a savings cushion that can cover unexpected expenses. Having an emergency fund helps prevent accumulating further debt in the event of unforeseen circumstances.

Exploring Debt Consolidation: Debt consolidation involves combining multiple debts into a single loan or credit account with a lower interest rate. This approach simplifies your repayment process by having only one monthly payment. It can also help lower your overall interest costs, making debt repayment more manageable. However, carefully evaluate the terms and costs associated with consolidation before proceeding.

Seeking Professional Guidance: If you're overwhelmed or struggling with debt management, consider seeking professional guidance. Financial advisors, credit counselors, or debt management agencies can provide expert advice tailored to your specific situation. They can help you develop a personalized plan, negotiate with creditors on your behalf, and provide ongoing support.

Monitoring Your Credit Score: Regularly monitoring your credit score is important for managing debt effectively. Your credit score impacts your ability to access credit in the future and may influence interest rates on loans or credit cards. Review your credit report annually, address any inaccuracies, and strive to maintain a good credit score through responsible debt management.

Staying Committed and Disciplined: Managing debt requires discipline and a long-term commitment. Stick to your budget, make consistent payments, and avoid incurring additional debt. Stay motivated by tracking your progress, celebrating milestones, and envisioning the financial freedom you will achieve once your debts are fully repaid. Remember, managing debt is not a quick fix but a gradual process that requires perseverance and responsible financial habits. By taking proactive steps and adopting smart strategies, you can regain control of your finances, reduce debt stress, and work towards a more stable and secure financial future.

THE KINGDOM OF FINANCIAL PLANNING

Financial planning is a comprehensive process that involves evaluating your current financial situation, setting financial goals, and developing a roadmap to achieve those goals. It encompasses various aspects of personal finance, including budgeting, saving, investing, retirement planning, risk management, and estate planning. Here, I will elaborate in greater detail on what financial planning entails towards building your kingdom:

Assessing Your Financial Situation: Financial planning begins with assessing your current financial situation. This includes evaluating your income, expenses, assets, liabilities, and net worth. Understanding your financial standing provides a baseline for setting realistic goals and making informed decisions.

Setting Financial Goals: Financial planning involves identifying short-term and long-term financial goals. Short-term goals may include creating an emergency fund, paying off debt, or saving for a specific purchase. Long-term goals typically revolve around retirement planning, education funding, homeownership, or wealth accumulation. Setting clear and measurable goals helps guide your financial planning process.

Creating a Budget: A budget is a crucial component of financial planning. It involves tracking your income and expenses to ensure your spending aligns with your financial goals. By creating a budget, you can identify areas where you can reduce expenses, allocate funds towards savings and investments, and avoid overspending.

Saving and Investment Strategies: Financial planning involves developing strategies to save and invest your money effectively. This includes setting aside a portion of your income for short-term and long-term savings goals. It also entails exploring different investment options, such as stocks, bonds, mutual funds, real estate, or retirement accounts, to grow your wealth over time.

Retirement Planning: A significant aspect of financial planning is preparing for retirement. This involves estimating your retirement expenses, determining the desired retirement age, and calculating the savings needed to maintain your desired lifestyle during retirement. Financial planners can help analyze your retirement needs, recommend suitable retirement accounts, and create a retirement savings strategy.

Risk Management and Insurance: Financial planning includes assessing and managing financial risks. This involves evaluating your insurance needs, such as health insurance, life insurance, disability insurance, or property insurance. Adequate insurance coverage protects you and your loved ones from unexpected expenses and financial hardships.

Tax Planning: Financial planning also incorporates tax planning strategies to optimize your tax efficiency. This may involve maximizing deductions and credits, utilizing tax-advantaged investment accounts, or implementing strategies to minimize taxable income. Consulting with a tax professional can help you navigate the complexities of tax planning.

Estate Planning: Estate planning is an integral part of financial planning, particularly for individuals with significant assets. It involves creating a plan for the distribution of your assets upon your death, minimizing estate taxes, and ensuring your wishes are carried out. Estate planning typically includes creating a will, establishing trusts, and designating beneficiaries.

Regular Monitoring and Review: Financial planning is not a one-time event but an ongoing process. Regularly monitor your progress towards your financial goals and adjust your plan as needed. Life circumstances, economic conditions, and personal goals may change over time, necessitating revisions to your financial plan.

Seeking Professional Advice: While you can create a financial plan on your own, consulting with a financial planner can provide valuable expertise and guidance. Financial planners can assess your financial situation, offer personalized recommendations, and help you make informed decisions aligned with your goals. Financial planning empowers individuals to take control of their financial future, make informed decisions, and work towards their desired financial outcomes. By developing a comprehensive financial plan and implementing appropriate strategies, you can increase your financial well-being, achieve your goals, and navigate through life's financial complexities with confidence.

THE KINGDOM OF RISK MANAGEMENT

Having insurance is a fundamental component of managing risk and protecting oneself against potential financial losses. Insurance provides a safety net that helps individuals, businesses, and organizations mitigate the financial impact of unforeseen events or accidents. Here, I will elaborate in greater detail the importance of insurance in managing risk towards building your ideal kingdom:

Types of Insurance: There are various types of insurance available to manage different risks:

a. Health Insurance: Health insurance covers medical expenses, including hospitalization, doctor visits, medications, and treatments. It helps individuals manage the high costs of healthcare and ensures access to necessary medical services.

b. Life Insurance: Life insurance provides financial protection to beneficiaries in the event of the policyholder's death. It helps replace lost income, pay off debts, cover funeral expenses, or fund future financial needs for dependents.

c. Property Insurance: Property insurance protects physical assets such as homes, vehicles, or businesses against damage or loss due to events like fire, theft, natural disasters, or accidents. It ensures financial support for repair or replacement costs.

d. Auto Insurance: Auto insurance provides coverage for damages or injuries resulting from automobile accidents. It protects vehicle owners from financial liability and may also offer coverage for theft or vandalism.

e. Liability Insurance: Liability insurance protects individuals or businesses from legal claims and financial obligations resulting from injuries or property damage caused to others. It includes general liability insurance, professional liability insurance, and product liability insurance.

f. Disability Insurance: Disability insurance provides income replacement if an individual becomes disabled and unable to work. It ensures a source of income to cover living expenses during a period of disability.

g. Long-Term Care Insurance: Long-term care insurance covers the costs associated with extended healthcare services, such as nursing home care, assisted living, or in-home care. It helps individuals cover expenses not typically covered by health insurance.

Financial Protection: Insurance provides financial protection against unexpected events or losses. By paying regular premiums, individuals transfer the risk of financial loss to the insurance company. In exchange, the insurer provides coverage and compensation for covered losses, reducing the financial burden on the policyholder.

Risk Transfer: Insurance allows individuals or businesses to transfer the risk of potential losses to the insurance provider. Instead of bearing the full financial consequences of an unfortunate event, policyholders pay a relatively small premium to shift the risk to the insurer. This helps protect personal assets, savings, or investments from being depleted by a significant loss.

Peace of Mind: Having insurance offers peace of mind by alleviating concerns about potential financial hardships. It provides a sense of security, knowing that there is a safety net in place to support individuals or businesses in times of crisis. This peace of mind allows individuals to focus on their daily activities and long-term goals without constant worry about unforeseen events.

Legal and Contractual Requirements: In many cases, insurance is required by law or contractual agreements. For example, auto insurance is mandatory in most jurisdictions to protect third parties from accidents caused by vehicle owners. Similarly, lenders may require borrowers to have property insurance when obtaining a mortgage to safeguard the property against potential damage or loss.

Business Continuity: For businesses, insurance plays a crucial role in ensuring continuity and minimizing disruptions. Business insurance covers risks such as property damage, liability claims, employee injuries, or interruption of operations due to unforeseen events. It helps businesses recover and resume normal operations after a loss, reducing financial strain and protecting their long-term viability.

Risk Management: Insurance is an essential component of overall risk management strategies. It allows individuals and businesses to assess potential risks, quantify them, and implement appropriate risk mitigation measures. Insurance acts as a safety net for risks that cannot be entirely eliminated, providing financial protection and minimizing the impact of adverse events.

Access to Resources: Access to resources refers to the availability, opportunity, and ability to obtain and utilize various types of assets or materials that are necessary for individuals, communities, or organizations to meet their needs, achieve their goals, and improve their well-being.

THE KINGDOM OF
INVESTING & WEALTH BUILDING

Building wealth and investing strategies are essential for achieving long-term financial goals and securing a stable financial future. Here, I will elaborate in greater detail on ways to build wealth and provide strategies for investing towards building your kingdom:

Live Below Your Means: Practice frugality and avoid excessive spending. Differentiate between needs and wants, and prioritize your financial goals over unnecessary expenses. By living below your means, you can free up more money to save and invest, accelerating your wealth-building journey.

Entrepreneurship: Starting a business can be a path to wealth-building. Identify a viable business opportunity, develop a solid business plan, and pursue your entrepreneurial aspirations. Entrepreneurship offers the potential for significant financial gains, but it also comes with risks, so thorough research and planning are crucial.

Increase Income: Increasing your income is a crucial step in building wealth. Explore opportunities for career advancement, acquire new skills, or consider additional sources of income such as a side business, freelancing, or passive income streams. By earning more, you have more funds available for saving and investing.

Establish a Budget: Building wealth starts with effective budgeting. Create a detailed budget that tracks your income and expenses. Allocate a portion of your income towards savings and investments. By carefully managing your expenses and living within your means, you can free up funds for wealth-building activities.

Save and Invest Early: Time is a critical factor in building wealth. Start saving and investing as early as possible to take advantage of compounding returns. Regularly set aside a portion of your income for savings and invest those savings in appropriate vehicles to grow your wealth over time.

Diversify Your Investments: Diversification is a key strategy for managing risk and maximizing returns. Spread your investments across different asset classes, such as stocks, bonds, real estate, and commodities. Within each asset class, diversify further by investing in various companies or properties. Diversification helps mitigate the impact of market fluctuations and reduces the risk associated with any single investment.

Take Advantage of Retirement Accounts: Maximize your contributions to retirement accounts such as 401(k)s, IRAs, or pension plans. These accounts offer tax advantages and compound growth over time. Contribute at least enough to receive any employer matching contributions, as it represents free money towards your retirement savings.

Invest in Stocks: Investing in stocks can provide significant long-term returns. Educate yourself about the stock market, assess your risk tolerance, and consider investing in individual stocks or exchange-traded funds (ETFs) that align with your investment goals. Alternatively, you can invest in low-cost index funds that provide broad market exposure.

Real Estate Investments: Real estate can be a lucrative investment strategy. Consider purchasing rental properties, commercial properties, or real estate investment trusts (REITs). Real estate investments can generate rental income, appreciate in value over time, and provide tax benefits.

Build an Emergency Fund: Establishing an emergency fund is essential for financial security and wealth building. Set aside three to six months' worth of living expenses in a liquid and easily accessible account. An emergency fund helps you navigate unexpected financial challenges without having to rely on high-interest debt or liquidating long-term investments.

Seek Professional Advice: Consider consulting with a financial advisor who can provide personalized guidance based on your financial situation and goals. A financial advisor can help you develop a comprehensive investment plan, navigate complex financial markets, and adjust your strategy as needed.

Continual Learning and Monitoring: Building wealth requires ongoing education and monitoring of your investments. Stay informed about market trends, economic indicators, and changes in investment regulations. Regularly review and rebalance your portfolio to ensure it aligns with your goals and risk tolerance.

Manage Risks: Building wealth involves managing risks effectively. Protect your investments and assets with appropriate insurance coverage, such as property insurance, liability insurance, or life insurance. Diversify your investments to reduce exposure to individual risks and consider utilizing stop-loss orders or other risk management tools when investing in the stock market.

Stay Disciplined and Patient: Building wealth is a long-term endeavor that requires discipline and patience. Stick to your investment plan, avoid impulsive decisions based on short-term market fluctuations, and resist the temptation to time the market. Stay focused on your goals and be prepared for market ups and downs along the way.

THE KINGDOM OF REAL ESTATE

Making money in real estate can be a lucrative endeavor, but it requires knowledge, research, and careful decision-making. Here, I will elaborate in greater detail on various strategies to make money in real estate for building your kingdom:

Rental Properties: Purchasing residential or commercial properties and renting them out is a common way to generate rental income. The rental income can provide a consistent cash flow and potential appreciation over time. To be successful, research the local rental market, analyze potential rental yields, and carefully screen tenants to ensure reliable rental payments.

Fix-and-Flip: This strategy involves buying distressed properties at a discounted price, renovating or improving them, and then selling them at a higher price. Successful fix-and-flip ventures require a keen eye for undervalued properties, accurate estimation of renovation costs, and knowledge of the local real estate market. Conduct thorough due diligence to ensure that the renovation costs and potential sale price justify the investment.

Real Estate Investment Trusts (REITs): REITs allow individuals to invest in real estate without directly owning properties. REITs are companies that own, operate, or finance income-generating real estate properties. By investing in REITs, individuals can earn income through dividends and benefit from potential property value appreciation.

Vacation Rentals: Purchasing properties in tourist destinations and renting them out as vacation rentals can be profitable. Research the demand for vacation rentals in the area, consider factors such as proximity to attractions, amenities, and local regulations. Effective marketing and management are crucial for success in this niche.

Real Estate Development: Real estate development involves acquiring land or existing properties and improving them for sale or lease. This strategy requires substantial capital, expertise in development processes, and thorough market analysis. It can be highly profitable but also carries significant risks and requires careful planning and execution.

Real Estate Crowdfunding: Real estate crowdfunding platforms allow investors to pool their funds to invest in real estate projects. These platforms provide access to a wider range of investment opportunities, including residential, commercial, and development projects. Investors can choose projects based on their risk appetite and investment goals.

Wholesaling: Wholesaling involves finding deeply discounted properties and assigning the purchase contract to another buyer for a fee. As a wholesaler, you act as a middleman connecting motivated sellers with investors looking for properties. Successful wholesaling requires effective marketing, negotiation skills, and a network of buyers and sellers.

Real Estate Investment Partnerships: Forming partnerships with other investors can provide access to larger real estate projects and diversify risk. In a partnership, individuals pool their financial resources and expertise to acquire and manage properties collectively. Partnerships can involve joint ventures, limited liability companies (LLCs), or real estate syndications.

Buy and Hold: This strategy involves purchasing properties with the intention of holding onto them for the long term, benefiting from rental income, and potential property appreciation. It requires careful property selection, thorough analysis of cash flow potential, and a focus on acquiring properties in desirable locations with growth potential.

Tax Liens and Deeds: Investing in tax liens or tax deeds can provide opportunities to acquire properties at a significantly discounted price. When property owners fail to pay their property taxes, the local government may auction off the tax lien or deed to investors. Successful participation in tax lien or deed auctions requires research, due diligence, and knowledge of local laws.

Commercial Real Estate: Investing in commercial properties such as office buildings, retail spaces, or industrial properties can offer higher rental income and potential capital appreciation. However, commercial real estate requires extensive market research, understanding of tenant demands, and thorough financial analysis.

Real Estate Investment Clubs: Joining a real estate investment club offers networking opportunities, educational resources, access to deals, and a supportive community. It can accelerate your learning, open doors to potential partnerships and investments, and provide valuable market insights. Consider joining a reputable investment club to tap into these benefits and enhance your real estate investing journey.

THE KINGDOM OF FINANCIAL LITERACY

Financial education and awareness refer to the knowledge, skills, and understanding of various financial concepts, strategies, and practices that enable individuals to make informed decisions about their personal finances. It involves developing a comprehensive understanding of financial principles, products, and systems to effectively manage money, build wealth, and make sound financial choices. Here, I will elaborate in greater detail on what financial education and awareness encompass towards building your kingdom:

Personal Financial Management: Financial education involves learning how to manage personal finances effectively. It includes budgeting, tracking expenses, and understanding cash flow. By acquiring these skills, individuals can make informed decisions about saving, spending, and investing, and develop strategies to achieve their financial goals.

Basic Financial Literacy: Financial education promotes basic financial literacy, which encompasses understanding key financial terms, concepts, and calculations. This includes knowledge of interest rates, inflation, compounding, credit scores, and financial statements. Basic financial literacy empowers individuals to navigate financial systems, read and understand financial documents, and make informed choices.

Investment Knowledge: Financial education provides individuals with knowledge about various investment options, including stocks, bonds, mutual funds, real estate, and retirement accounts. It covers concepts such as risk and return, asset allocation, diversification, and the importance of long-term investing. With investment knowledge, individuals can make informed decisions to grow their wealth and achieve financial goals.

Debt Management: Financial education includes understanding the implications of borrowing money, managing debt effectively, and making informed decisions about credit. It involves learning about different types of debt, interest rates, repayment strategies, and debt consolidation. By acquiring debt management skills, individuals can avoid excessive debt, minimize interest payments, and maintain a healthy credit profile.

Retirement Planning: Financial education emphasizes the importance of retirement planning and understanding retirement accounts, such as 401(k)s, IRAs, and pension plans. It covers topics such as contribution limits, employer matching, investment options, and tax advantages. By being knowledgeable about retirement planning, individuals can make informed decisions to secure their financial future.

Risk Management and Insurance: Financial education includes understanding risk management and the role of insurance in protecting against financial uncertainties. It covers various types of insurance, such as health insurance, life insurance, property insurance, and liability insurance. By understanding insurance options and assessing individual needs, individuals can make informed decisions to mitigate risks and protect their assets.

Taxation and Tax Planning: Financial education encompasses understanding tax systems, tax obligations, and tax planning strategies. It includes knowledge of tax deductions, credits, and exemptions. By understanding taxation, individuals can optimize their tax positions, maximize tax savings, and comply with tax regulations.

Consumer Awareness: Financial education promotes consumer awareness and understanding of financial products and services. It involves knowing how to compare financial products, read contracts and agreements, and avoid scams and fraudulent activities. With consumer awareness, individuals can make informed choices when selecting financial institutions, investment products, or financial advisors.

Estate Planning: Financial education includes knowledge of estate planning and understanding the importance of wills, trusts, and powers of attorney. It covers concepts such as asset distribution, minimizing taxes, and ensuring the smooth transfer of wealth. With estate planning knowledge, individuals can protect their assets, provide for their loved ones, and plan for their legacy.

Continuous Learning: Financial education is an ongoing process that requires staying updated on financial trends, regulations, and market developments. It involves reading financial literature, attending workshops or seminars, and seeking advice from financial professionals. Continuous learning ensures individuals can adapt to changing financial landscapes and make informed decisions. By promoting financial education and awareness, individuals can enhance their financial well-being, make sound financial decisions, and work towards achieving their long-term financial goals.

THE KINGDOM OF INVESTING

Investing in the stock market can be an effective way to grow wealth and achieve long-term financial goals. However, for beginners, the prospect of entering the complex world of stocks may seem daunting. This comprehensive guide aims to provide a step-by-step approach to help you get started with stock market investing.

Educate Yourself: Before diving into the stock market, it's essential to build a solid foundation of knowledge. Familiarize yourself with basic investing concepts, such as stocks, bonds, mutual funds, and exchange-traded funds (ETFs). Learn about key financial ratios, market trends, and different investment strategies. Resources like books, online courses, investment websites, and financial news outlets can provide valuable educational material.

Define Your Investment Goals: Clarify your investment objectives to determine the appropriate investment strategy. Are you investing for retirement, saving for a down payment on a house, or aiming for long-term wealth accumulation? Each goal may have different timeframes and risk tolerance levels, which will influence your investment decisions.

Assess Risk Tolerance: Understanding your risk tolerance is crucial when investing in stocks. Evaluate how much risk you are comfortable taking on and how it aligns with your investment goals. Conservative investors may opt for a more stable approach, while aggressive investors may be willing to tolerate higher volatility for potentially higher returns.

Establish an Emergency Fund: Before investing, ensure you have a financial safety net in place. Set aside three to six months' worth of living expenses in a liquid and easily accessible emergency fund. This will protect you from unforeseen circumstances and allow you to invest with peace of mind.

Start with Retirement Accounts: Take advantage of tax-advantaged retirement accounts such as employer-sponsored 401(k) plans or individual retirement accounts (IRAs). These accounts offer tax benefits and can be a great starting point for long-term investing. Contribute regularly and consider maximizing your contributions to benefit from employer matches or tax deductions.

Determine your Investment Capital: Decide how much money you can afford to invest. Consider your financial obligations, debt repayments, and living expenses. It's crucial not to invest money that you might need in the short term, as the stock market can be volatile.

Choose a Brokerage Account: Select a reputable brokerage firm that aligns with your investing goals. Look for a platform that offers low trading fees, a user-friendly interface, educational resources, and research tools. Ensure the brokerage is regulated and provides a secure trading environment.

Research and Select Stocks: Before buying individual stocks, conduct thorough research. Analyze company fundamentals, financial statements, growth prospects, and industry trends. Consider diversifying your portfolio by investing in different sectors to mitigate risk. You can also explore investing in low-cost index funds or ETFs for broader market exposure.

Dollar-Cost Averaging: Implement a dollar-cost averaging strategy by investing a fixed amount regularly. This approach allows you to buy more shares when prices are low and fewer shares when prices are high. Over time, this can smooth out market volatility and potentially lead to favorable long-term returns.

Monitor and Rebalance: Regularly review your portfolio and make necessary adjustments based on changing market conditions and your investment goals. Rebalance your portfolio periodically to maintain your desired asset allocation. Avoid making emotional decisions based on short-term market fluctuations.

Stay Informed: Continuously educate yourself about market trends, economic indicators, and company news. Stay updated with financial publications, earnings reports, and reputable investment websites. Knowledge empowers you to make informed decisions and adapt to market dynamics.

Seek Professional Advice:
Consider consulting a financial advisor, especially if you have complex financial needs or a substantial portfolio. A professional advisor can help you develop a comprehensive investment strategy.

THE KINGDOM OF INVESTING

Investing in the stock market can be an effective way to grow wealth and achieve long-term financial goals. However, for beginners, the prospect of entering the complex world of stocks may seem daunting. This comprehensive guide aims to provide a step-by-step approach to help you get started with stock market investing.

Educate Yourself: Before diving into the stock market, it's essential to build a solid foundation of knowledge. Familiarize yourself with basic investing concepts, such as stocks, bonds, mutual funds, and exchange-traded funds (ETFs). Learn about key financial ratios, market trends, and different investment strategies. Resources like books, online courses, investment websites, and financial news outlets can provide valuable educational material.

Define Your Investment Goals: Clarify your investment objectives to determine the appropriate investment strategy. Are you investing for retirement, saving for a down payment on a house, or aiming for long-term wealth accumulation? Each goal may have different timeframes and risk tolerance levels, which will influence your investment decisions.

Assess Risk Tolerance: Understanding your risk tolerance is crucial when investing in stocks. Evaluate how much risk you are comfortable taking on and how it aligns with your investment goals. Conservative investors may opt for a more stable approach, while aggressive investors may be willing to tolerate higher volatility for potentially higher returns.

Establish an Emergency Fund: Before investing, ensure you have a financial safety net in place. Set aside three to six months' worth of living expenses in a liquid and easily accessible emergency fund. This will protect you from unforeseen circumstances and allow you to invest with peace of mind.

Start with Retirement Accounts: Take advantage of tax-advantaged retirement accounts such as employer-sponsored 401(k) plans or individual retirement accounts (IRAs). These accounts offer tax benefits and can be a great starting point for long-term investing. Contribute regularly and consider maximizing your contributions to benefit from employer matches or tax deductions.

Determine your Investment Capital: Decide how much money you can afford to invest. Consider your financial obligations, debt repayments, and living expenses. It's crucial not to invest money that you might need in the short term, as the stock market can be volatile.

Choose a Brokerage Account: Select a reputable brokerage firm that aligns with your investing goals. Look for a platform that offers low trading fees, a user-friendly interface, educational resources, and research tools. Ensure the brokerage is regulated and provides a secure trading environment.

Research and Select Stocks: Before buying individual stocks, conduct thorough research. Analyze company fundamentals, financial statements, growth prospects, and industry trends. Consider diversifying your portfolio by investing in different sectors to mitigate risk. You can also explore investing in low-cost index funds or ETFs for broader market exposure.

Dollar-Cost Averaging: Implement a dollar-cost averaging strategy by investing a fixed amount regularly. This approach allows you to buy more shares when prices are low and fewer shares when prices are high. Over time, this can smooth out market volatility and potentially lead to favorable long-term returns.

Monitor and Rebalance: Regularly review your portfolio and make necessary adjustments based on changing market conditions and your investment goals. Rebalance your portfolio periodically to maintain your desired asset allocation. Avoid making emotional decisions based on short-term market fluctuations.

Stay Informed: Continuously educate yourself about market trends, economic indicators, and company news. Stay updated with financial publications, earnings reports, and reputable investment websites. Knowledge empowers you to make informed decisions and adapt to market dynamics.

Seek Professional Advice:
Consider consulting a financial advisor, especially if you have complex financial needs or a substantial portfolio. A professional advisor can help you develop a comprehensive investment strategy.

THE KINGDOM OF TRUSTS

Trusts are versatile legal tools that enable individuals to protect and manage their assets, provide for their loved ones, and achieve specific financial goals. By establishing a trust, you can have greater control over your assets, mitigate taxes, avoid probate, and ensure your wealth is distributed according to your wishes. This article aims to provide a comprehensive overview of trusts, including different types, their benefits, and the steps involved in establishing a trust.

I. Trusts: An Overview

A trust is a legal arrangement where a person (the settlor or grantor) transfers assets to a trustee, who holds and manages those assets on behalf of the beneficiaries. Trusts can be revocable or irrevocable, meaning the settlor may retain control over the assets or relinquish control once established.

Do I need a trust? Trusts aren't just for rich people. They can be an important part of estate planning and can provide peace of mind by ensuring your assets will go to the right people. Certain types of trusts allow you to avoid having your estate go through probate, which is a court-supervised process of determining the validity of your will (if you have one) and distributing your assets after death. That process can take several months, and much of it is public record. Trusts can be made by consulting with an estate planning attorney, using DIY estate planning software or using estate planning programs provided by your workplace.

Who is involved in a trust? Trusts have three main players:
Grantor: The person who creates the trust and puts assets in it.

Beneficiary: A person who eventually receives some or all of the assets in the trust.
Trustee: The organization or person who administers the trust.

Advantages of a trust
Effectiveness: The main purpose of a trust is to transfer assets from one person to another. Trusts can hold different kinds of assets. Investment accounts, houses and cars are examples.

Control: You can specify the terms of the trust, which means a trust can help you be strategic if you want to protect assets after a divorce, for example, or control when kids get your money, or control how people spend the money you leave them.

Privacy: Assets in living trusts don't have to go through probate. That process is public record, which can create drama if you're disinheriting someone or making distributions that you don't want to be public.

Time: Probate can take several months. Trusts can avoid probate and get assets to your heirs faster.

Potential tax savings: Some types of trusts can lower your estate taxes. However, most people don't have to pay estate taxes, so talk with a financial advisor before setting up a trust. There's no reason to use a trust to avoid taxes you may not have to pay anyway.

Disadvantages of a trust

Cost: An estate planning attorney can do the paperwork involved in setting up a trust and transferring your assets into the trust, but hiring one can cost upward of $1,000. Online will makers are available, but many aren't able to create trusts.

Time: You'll need to spend time dealing with paperwork. You may need to have uncomfortable conversations about who gets what.

May not be necessary for tax reasons: Some people can indeed save on estate taxes with certain trusts, but most estates aren't subject to estate taxes in the first place.

Taxes and trusts

This is a complicated area of the tax code, so be sure to consult with a qualified professional. Here are a few things to keep in mind:

Estate taxes: If you have a large estate, your assets may be subject to federal estate tax when you die. The federal estate tax ranges from rates of 18% to 40% and generally only applies to assets over $12.06 million in 2022 or $12.92 million in 2023. Also, some states have their own estate taxes (and set their own estate size thresholds), so there could be two estate tax bills to pay.

Inheritance taxes: Some states have inheritance taxes, which are different from estate taxes. The people who inherit the money pay the tax.

Income taxes: The assets in a trust might generate income, which could trigger income taxe or capital gains taxes. Who pays that tax depends on who legally owns the assets. If a charity gets the income directly, that donation might qualify for a tax deduction.

Time and effort: You may have some extra paperwork to do at tax time because trusts sometimes have to file their own tax returns.

Types of trusts
You can tailor a trust to your needs. As such, there arc a variety of different types of trusts to choose from, but all trusts fall under two main categories: Revocable & Irrevocable.

1. Revocable trusts
Revocable trusts, also referred to as living trusts, are created during the grantor's lifetime and are generally used for:

Planning for incapacitation: If you're diagnosed with a debilitating condition, you can get things in order before you're unable to do so. When that day comes, the successor trustee takes over managing the trust assets for you.

Avoiding probate: Assets in a revocable trust can bypass probate — the time-consuming process of settling an estate. Assets that pass through probate become public record, so bypassing probate can be beneficial if you'd prefer to keep the details of the trust private. In a revocable trust, you (the grantor) can change the beneficiaries and assets as long as you're alive and physically and mentally able to do so. You can even name yourself as the trustee and name a co-trustee or successor trustee. However, revocable trusts do not include any tax benefits or protection from creditors. For that, you may want to consider an irrevocable trust.

Benefits:
a. Probate avoidance: Assets held in a revocable living trust can bypass the probate process, saving time and costs.

b. Privacy: Unlike a will, a trust's terms and asset distribution are generally not public.
c. Incapacity planning: A successor trustee can seamlessly manage the trust assets if the settlor becomes incapacitated.

d. Flexibility: The settlor can make changes to the trust terms during their lifetime.

2. Irrevocable trusts
Irrevocable trusts are often used to minimize estate taxes for beneficiaries. In an irrevocable trust, you can't change your mind. Once you put assets in the trust and name a beneficiary, it's permanent. An advantage of irrevocable trusts is that you might be

able to reduce your estate taxes because the assets in an irrevocable trust technically aren't yours anymore. The trust owns them.

These trusts are typically used: To receive and hold assets after the grantor dies. To hold lifetime gifts for the grantor's heirs or beneficiaries.

Benefits:
a. Asset protection: By removing assets from your estate, they are shielded from creditors or legal claims.

b. Estate tax planning: Irrevocable trusts can help minimize estate taxes by transferring assets to beneficiaries while you are still alive.

c. Medicaid planning: Transferring assets to an irrevocable trust may help you qualify for Medicaid benefits while preserving some wealth for your heirs.

d. Charitable giving: Charitable trusts allow you to support causes you care about while providing potential tax benefits.

Let's explore various types of trusts:
Testamentary Trust:
A testamentary trust is established through a will and only takes effect upon the settlor's death. It allows the settlor to provide for beneficiaries who may be minors, disabled, or require guidance in managing their inheritance.

Benefits:

a. Protection for beneficiaries: Testamentary trusts provide safeguards for beneficiaries who may not be ready to manage their inheritance.

b. Control over distribution: You can specify how and when the assets will be distributed to beneficiaries.

c. Tax planning: Testamentary trusts can help minimize estate taxes and preserve wealth for future generations.

Grantor retained annuity trust (GRAT): Allows the grantor to direct certain assets into a temporary trust and freeze its value, removing additional appreciation from the estate and giving it to heirs with minimal estate or gift tax liability.

Education trust: Beneficiaries can only use the money for educational expenses.

Spendthrift trust: When beneficiaries can't make good financial decisions for themselves, the trustee decides how the beneficiary is allowed to use the money.

Charitable trust: An irrevocable trust from which you leave a bequest of assets to one or more charities.

Functional-needs trust: For families with children who have functional needs, these trusts set specific rules for how the money will go to the beneficiary.

Qualified personal residence trust: An irrevocable trust in which you transfer a house to your heirs but get to live in it for a specified period first.

Qualified terminable interest property (QTIP) trust: When the first spouse dies, the trust supports the surviving spouse; when the surviving spouse dies, the remaining assets go solely to the first spouse's chosen beneficiaries.

Generation-skipping trusts: A trust in which you transfer money to grandchildren or other people who are at least 37.5 years younger than you.

II. Establishing a Trust:
Establishing a trust involves several key steps:

Determine your objectives: Clarify your goals, such as asset protection, estate tax planning, or providing for loved ones, to determine the appropriate trust type. Determine what kind of trust best fits your needs. It's a good idea to consult with an estate planning attorney about your requirements.

Choose a trustee: Select a trustworthy individual, institution, or professional trustee to manage the trust according to your wishes.

Create the trust agreement: Consult with an attorney experienced in estate planning to draft a comprehensive trust agreement that outlines the trust's terms, asset distribution, and trustee's responsibilities.

Create a trust document: Your attorney will help you do this. Or, if you're setting up the trust through an online DIY service, most companies will provide some online guidance to help you through the process.

Get it signed and notarized: Depending on your state laws, you may need multiple signatures from the grantor(s) and trustee(s), and you might also need witnesses during the process.

Open a trust account: Trusts can hold many different types of assets, including cash, stocks, bonds, mutual funds, real estate and other property.

Fund the trust: Transfer assets into the trust by changing ownership or titling them in the trust's name. This step varies depending on the type of assets, such as real estate, bank accounts, or investment accounts. Transfer assets into the trust. However, if the trust is established as part of an estate plan, you can designate the trust as a beneficiary so that the assets move to the trust once the grantor passes away.

Appoint successor trustees and beneficiaries: Designate successor trustees who will assume control if the initial trustee is unable or unwilling to serve. Clearly identify the beneficiaries who will receive the trust assets. Consult with an estate planning attorney. Fees can vary widely, but professional guidance is often worth it. An estate planning attorney can draft your trust documents according to your requirements.

DIY: Some websites offer "do-it-yourself" trusts. They may be a low-cost option, but you may pay in time and effort.

Do it through work: Some companies offer discounted estate planning services as part of their employee benefits packages.

Trusts can be complex and intricate, so if you're unsure about the best choices for you and your family, consult with a legal or financial professional before making a decision.

Review and update regularly: Regularly review your trust to ensure it aligns with your current circumstances, and make necessary amendments if there are any changes in your family, financial situation, or goals.

Trusts are powerful estate planning tools that offer numerous benefits, including asset protection, probate avoidance, tax planning, and control over asset distribution. By understanding the different types of trusts and their respective advantages, you can make informed decisions about establishing a trust that aligns with your goals and protects your legacy. Consulting with an experienced attorney is crucial to navigate the legal complexities and tailor a trust to your unique needs.

THE KINGDOM OF WILLS

Wills are fundamental estate planning tools that allow individuals to control the distribution of their assets and express their final wishes. A well-drafted will ensures that your loved ones are taken care of and your estate is managed according to your instructions. This article aims to provide a comprehensive overview of wills, including different types, their benefits, and the steps involved in establishing a will.

Wills: A will is a legal document that outlines how you want your assets to be distributed after your death. It appoints an executor to carry out your wishes and may also include provisions for guardianship of minor children. Let's explore various types of wills:

Simple Will: A simple will is a basic document that outlines your wishes regarding the distribution of your assets. It is suitable for individuals with uncomplicated estates and straightforward distribution plans.

Benefits:
a. Asset distribution: A simple will ensures that your assets go to the beneficiaries of your choice.
b. Appointment of executor: You can designate a trusted individual to manage your estate and handle the distribution process.
c. Guardianship provisions: If you have minor children, a simple will allows you to name a guardian to care for them in the event of your passing.

Testamentary Trust Will: A testamentary trust will includes provisions for creating one or more trusts upon your death. This type of will is particularly useful when dealing with complex family dynamics or when beneficiaries require additional guidance or protection.

Benefits:
a. Flexibility and control: By establishing trusts, you have control over how and when your assets are distributed to beneficiaries, even after your passing.
b. Asset protection: Trusts can safeguard assets for beneficiaries who may be minors, financially irresponsible, or in need of long-term care.
c. Tax planning: Testamentary trusts can help minimize estate taxes and preserve wealth for future generations.
d. Special needs planning: Testamentary trusts allow you to provide for loved ones with special needs without jeopardizing their eligibility for government benefits.

Living Will: A living will, also known as an advance healthcare directive, is a document that outlines your preferences for medical treatment in the event you become unable to communicate your wishes.

Benefits:
a. Medical decision-making: A living will ensures that your healthcare preferences are honored, even if you cannot express them at the time.
b. Relieves burden on loved ones: By clearly stating your medical treatment desires, you alleviate the burden of decision-making from your family during emotionally challenging times.
c. Ensures dignity and respect: A living will allows you to maintain control over your medical care and ensure your values and beliefs are respected.

Establishing a Will:
Establishing a will involves several key steps:

Determine your wishes: Make a comprehensive list of your assets, including property, investments, bank accounts, and personal belongings. Determine how you want these assets to be distributed.

Appoint an executor: Choose a trustworthy individual or professional executor who will be responsible for administering your estate and carrying out your wishes.

Seek professional assistance: Consult with an experienced estate planning attorney to draft your will. They will ensure that your will meets all legal requirements and accurately reflects your intentions.

Include necessary provisions: Specify how you want your assets to be distributed, appoint guardians for minor children if applicable, and address any specific wishes you may have.

Sign and witness the will: Sign your will in the presence of witnesses who are not beneficiaries or related to beneficiaries. The number of witnesses required varies by jurisdiction.

Keep the will safe: Store your original will in a secure location, such as a safe deposit box or with your attorney, and inform your loved ones about its whereabouts.

Regularly review and update: Review your will periodically, especially after major life events such as marriage, divorce, the birth of children, or significant changes in your financial situation.

Wills are vital tools for estate planning, allowing you to ensure the smooth distribution of your assets, appoint guardians for minor children, and express your healthcare preferences. By understanding the different types of wills and their respective benefits, you can make informed decisions about establishing a will that aligns with your goals and protects your loved ones. It is crucial to consult with an experienced estate planning attorney to navigate the legal complexities and draft a will that accurately reflects your wishes.

THE 2ND JEWEL: ASSET OWNERSHIP

Asset ownership refers to the legal possession and control of an asset. An asset is anything of value that can be owned or controlled and has the potential to generate income or appreciate in value over time. Assets can include physical property, jewelry, land, art, financial instruments, intellectual property, businesses, or other forms of wealth. Here, I will elaborate in greater detail on the concept of asset ownership towards building a strong kingdom:

Types of Assets: Assets can be classified into different categories based on their nature and characteristics. These categories include:

a. Tangible Assets: These are physical assets that have a physical form and can be touched or seen. Examples include real estate, vehicles, machinery, equipment, and inventory.

b. Financial Assets: Financial assets are intangible assets that represent ownership of a claim to future cash flows or financial benefits. Examples include stocks, bonds, mutual funds, certificates of deposit (CDs), and bank accounts.

c. Intellectual Property: Intellectual property refers to intangible assets resulting from human creativity and innovation. It includes books, music, patents, trademarks, copyrights, and trade secrets.

d. Business Ownership: Owning a business or shares in a business constitutes ownership of an asset. This can include sole proprietorships, partnerships, or ownership of shares in corporations.

THE KINGDOM OF ASSETS

Benefits of Asset Ownership: Owning assets can provide several benefits, including:

a. Wealth Accumulation: Assets have the potential to appreciate in value over time, enabling individuals to accumulate wealth. Appreciation can occur due to market conditions, improvements, or increased demand for the asset.

b. Income Generation: Certain assets, such as rental properties, businesses, or dividend-paying stocks, can generate regular income streams. This income can contribute to financial stability and serve as a passive source of cash flow.

c. Portfolio Diversification: Owning a diverse range of assets can help spread risk and reduce exposure to any single asset or sector. Diversification can protect against market volatility and enhance long-term investment returns.

d. Control and Flexibility: Asset ownership provides individuals with control over their assets. They can make decisions regarding how the asset is managed, utilized, or transferred. Ownership offers flexibility in adapting to changing circumstances and financial goals.

e. Collateral for Financing: Assets can be used as collateral to secure loans or lines of credit. Lenders may be more willing to extend credit when there is an asset to serve as collateral, allowing individuals to access additional funds for personal or business needs.

Legal Aspects of Asset Ownership: Asset ownership involves legal rights and responsibilities. Ownership is established through legal documents, such as property deeds, vehicle titles, stock certificates, or business registration documents. Legal ownership provides individuals with the right to use, sell, transfer, or dispose of the asset according to applicable laws and regulations.

Risks and Responsibilities: Asset ownership also comes with risks and responsibilities. These may include market volatility, maintenance and upkeep costs, regulatory compliance, insurance obligations, and tax implications. Owners must be aware of these risks and take appropriate measures to mitigate them.

Estate Planning: Asset ownership is a critical component of estate planning. Individuals need to consider how their assets will be transferred or distributed upon their death. Estate planning involves creating wills, trusts, or other legal mechanisms to ensure the orderly transfer of assets to beneficiaries and minimize potential disputes. It's important for individuals to understand the nature of their assets, their rights and responsibilities as owners, and the potential benefits and risks associated with asset ownership. This knowledge enables individuals to make informed decisions, effectively manage their assets, and work towards their financial goals.

ASSETS VS. LIABILITIES

Appreciable Assets Versus Liabilities: Here is a more detailed explanation of the types of assets that appreciate in value versus liabilities. Assets will clearly help you build a more stable kingdom:

ASSETS THAT APPRECIATE
Real Estate: Real estate is one of the most common assets that tends to appreciate over time. The value of properties can increase due to factors such as location, demand, improvements, and market conditions. Investing in residential, commercial, or rental properties can provide long-term appreciation and potential rental income.

Stocks and Equities: Investing in stocks and equities of well-established companies can offer the potential for capital appreciation. The value of stocks can increase as the company grows, generates profits, and attracts investor confidence. However, stock values can also fluctuate and are subject to market volatility.

Bonds: Certain types of bonds, such as government or corporate bonds, can appreciate over time. Bonds are debt instruments that pay periodic interest and return the principal upon maturity. If interest rates decrease or the issuer's credit rating improves, the value of existing bonds can rise.

Mutual Funds and Exchange-Traded Funds (ETFs): Mutual funds and ETFs pool investors' money to invest in a diversified portfolio of assets. These funds can include stocks, bonds, and other securities. When the underlying assets appreciate, the value of the mutual fund or ETF shares can increase.

Art, Collectibles, and Antiques: Certain forms of art, collectibles, and antiques can appreciate in value, particularly if they are rare, in demand, or associated with well-known artists or historical significance. However, the value of such assets can be subjective and may fluctuate based on changing trends and market demand.

Intellectual Property: Intellectual property assets, such as patents, trademarks, and copyrights, can appreciate in value over time. These assets can generate royalties or licensing fees and may increase in worth if they are in high demand or subject to potential commercialization.

LIABILITIES

Loans and Debts: Liabilities generally refer to debts or financial obligations that need to be repaid. This can include mortgage loans, credit card debt, personal loans, or auto loans. Unlike assets, liabilities typically do not appreciate in value and can carry interest charges, making them costly to maintain.

Depreciating Assets: Some assets may depreciate over time, meaning their value decreases rather than appreciates. This can include vehicles, certain types of equipment, or technology that becomes outdated. Depreciating assets may require ongoing maintenance and can result in financial losses when sold.

Consumer Goods: Consumer goods, such as electronics, furniture, or clothing, are typically considered liabilities as they tend to depreciate in value after purchase. These items often have limited resale value and may become outdated or worn out over time. It's important to note that the distinction between assets and liabilities can depend on various factors, such as market conditions, specific assets' performance, and individual financial goals. Additionally, some assets can have both appreciation potential and liabilities associated with their ownership, such as real estate properties that require ongoing maintenance costs. It's advisable to carefully evaluate the characteristics and potential risks associated with each asset or liability before making investment or financial decisions.

THE KINGDOM OF HOME OWNERHSIP

Benefits of Owning A Home: Home ownership offers several benefits that go beyond having a place to live. Here, I will elaborate in greater detail on the advantages of home ownership:

Building Equity: One of the primary benefits of home ownership is the opportunity to build equity. Equity is the difference between the market value of a property and the remaining mortgage balance. As you make mortgage payments over time, you increase your equity in the home. Building equity can be seen as a form of forced savings, as you are gradually building wealth through property ownership.

Appreciation: Historically, real estate has shown a tendency to appreciate in value over the long term. While there are no guarantees, owning a home gives you the potential to benefit from property value appreciation. As the value of your home increases, so does your net worth. Appreciation can be influenced by factors such as location, economic conditions, and market demand.

Stability and Security: Home ownership provides stability and a sense of security. When you own a home, you have more control over your living environment. You don't have to worry about rent increases or the possibility of being asked to move by a landlord. Having a stable home can provide a sense of belonging, community, and emotional well-being.

Control over the Property: When you own a home, you have the freedom to make modifications and improvements according to your preferences. You can customize the property to suit your needs, whether it's renovating the kitchen, creating a beautiful garden, or adding extra rooms. This level of control allows you to create a living space that truly reflects your style and enhances your quality of life.

Tax Benefits: Homeownership often comes with various tax benefits. In many countries, homeowners can deduct mortgage interest payments and property taxes from their taxable income. These deductions can reduce the overall tax burden, providing potential savings. Additionally, when selling a primary residence, there may be tax advantages such as capital gains exclusions, depending on local tax laws.

Stability of Monthly Housing Costs: Unlike renting, where landlords can increase rent prices, owning a home provides stability in monthly housing costs. If you have a fixed-rate mortgage, your principal and interest payments remain consistent throughout the loan term, allowing you to budget more effectively.

This predictability can provide financial peace of mind and make long-term financial planning easier.

Borrowing Power: Homeownership can enhance your borrowing power. As you build equity in your home, you may have the option to borrow against it through a home equity loan or line of credit. These loans can be used for various purposes, such as home improvements, education expenses, or debt consolidation. Owning a home can provide you with a valuable asset that can be leveraged to access additional funds if needed.

Pride of Ownership: Owning a home often brings a sense of pride and accomplishment. It gives you the opportunity to establish roots, create memories, and be part of a community. Homeownership can provide a sense of stability, independence, and a place to call your own. It's important to note that homeownership also comes with responsibilities, such as property maintenance, repairs, and associated costs. Additionally, the benefits of homeownership can vary depending on individual circumstances, market conditions, and location. It's advisable to carefully consider your financial situation, long-term plans, and consult with professionals before making the decision to purchase a home.

THE KINGDOM OF OWNERSHIP VS RENTING

Pros & Cons of Home Ownership Versus Renting

Here is a more detailed exploration of the pros and cons of owning a home versus renting in building your kingdom:

PROS OF OWNING A HOME

Equity and Investment: Homeownership allows you to build equity over time. As you pay down your mortgage and the property value appreciates, you are essentially building wealth through ownership.

Stability and Control: Owning a home provides stability and control over your living situation. You can customize and modify the property to suit your preferences, and you are not subject to the whims of a landlord.

Tax Benefits: Homeowners can take advantage of tax benefits such as deductions for mortgage interest and property taxes, potentially reducing their overall tax liability.

Pride of Ownership: Owning a home can give you a sense of pride and accomplishment. It offers the opportunity to establish roots, create a sense of community, and enjoy the benefits of homeownership.

Potential for Rental Income: If you have extra space, such as a basement or additional unit, you can potentially generate rental income by leasing it out, providing an additional revenue stream.

CONS OF OWNING A HOME

Financial Commitment: Homeownership requires a significant financial commitment. It involves upfront costs such as down payment, closing costs, and ongoing expenses like mortgage payments, property taxes, insurance, maintenance, and repairs.

Lack of Flexibility: Owning a home can limit your flexibility to move. Selling a property can take time and is subject to market conditions, which can restrict your ability to relocate quickly.

Maintenance and Repairs: As a homeowner, you are responsible for the maintenance and repairs of the property. This includes regular upkeep, unexpected repairs, and associated costs, which can add up over time.

Market Risk: The value of a property can fluctuate based on economic conditions and market trends. There is a possibility that your property may depreciate, impacting your overall investment.

PROS OF RENTING

Flexibility: Renting provides more flexibility and mobility. It allows you to easily move locations or adjust your living situation based on your changing needs and circumstances.

Lower Initial Costs: Renting typically requires lower upfront costs compared to homeownership. You generally need to pay a security deposit and possibly some utilities, making it more accessible for those with limited savings.

Limited Responsibilities: As a renter, you are not responsible for major repairs or maintenance of the property. These tasks are typically the landlord's responsibility, freeing you from the financial and time commitments associated with homeownership.

Access to Amenities: Rental properties often come with amenities such as gyms, pools, and shared spaces that may be costly or unavailable to homeowners.

CONS OF RENTING

No Equity Building: Unlike owning a home, renting does not offer the opportunity to build equity. Rent payments contribute solely to the landlord's income rather than building your personal wealth.

Lack of Control and Customization: Renting restricts your ability to make changes to the property. You must adhere to the landlord's rules and obtain permission for any modifications or improvements.

Rent Increases: Rental prices can fluctuate over time, subject to market conditions and the landlord's discretion. This lack of control can make budgeting for the long term more challenging.

Limited Stability: Renting provides less stability compared to homeownership. Landlords may decide not to renew your lease, potentially forcing you to find a new place to live. It's important to consider these factors based on your individual circumstances, financial goals, and lifestyle preferences. Renting may be more suitable for those who prioritize flexibility and lower upfront costs, while homeownership can be appealing for those seeking long-term stability, wealth building, and control over their living environment.

THE KINGDOM OF CREDIT

Your credit score is a crucial financial asset that impacts your ability to secure loans, obtain favorable interest rates, and achieve financial goals. Taking proactive steps to protect and improve your credit is essential for long-term financial success. This comprehensive guide will provide you with valuable insights and actionable tips to safeguard your credit and enhance your creditworthiness.

Monitor Your Credit Reports Regularly: Obtain copies of your credit reports from the major credit bureaus (Equifax, Experian, and TransUnion) at least once a year. Review them carefully to ensure accuracy and detect any errors or fraudulent activities. If you identify any discrepancies, promptly dispute them with the respective credit bureaus.

Pay Your Bills on Time: Consistently paying your bills on time is one of the most critical factors affecting your credit score. Set up payment reminders, automate your payments, or create a budgeting system to ensure you never miss a payment. Late payments can have a significant negative impact on your credit score.

Maintain a Low Credit Utilization Ratio: Your credit utilization ratio refers to the amount of available credit you are using. Aim to keep this ratio below 30%. High credit utilization can signal financial strain and negatively impact your credit score. Pay off debts, reduce credit card balances, and avoid maxing out your credit cards to maintain a healthy credit utilization ratio.

Build a Solid Credit History: A longer credit history demonstrates your ability to manage credit responsibly. If you're new to credit, consider obtaining a secured credit card or becoming an authorized user on a family member's credit card to start building credit. Ensure you make timely payments and keep your credit utilization low.

Avoid Frequent Credit Applications: Each time you apply for credit, it triggers a hard inquiry on your credit report. Multiple hard inquiries within a short period can signal financial distress and lower your credit score. Apply for credit only when necessary and avoid opening multiple new accounts simultaneously.

Diversify Your Credit Mix: Having a diverse range of credit accounts, such as credit cards, mortgages, and installment loans, can positively impact your credit score. However, avoid opening new accounts solely for the sake of diversification. Only pursue credit that you genuinely need and can manage responsibly.

Don't Close Old Credit Accounts: Closing old credit accounts may seem like a logical step, but it can potentially harm your credit score. Lengthy credit history is beneficial, and closing old accounts shortens your credit history. If you decide to close an account, focus on paying off existing debts and keeping your credit utilization low.

Use Credit Monitoring and Identity Theft Protection Services: Consider enrolling in credit monitoring and identity theft protection services. These services can alert you to any suspicious activity on your credit file, monitor your credit score, and provide tools to resolve identity theft issues promptly.

Be Cautious with Co-signing: Co-signing a loan makes you equally responsible for the debt. Think carefully before agreeing to be a co-signer, as any default or late payment by the primary borrower can damage your credit. Only co-sign for individuals you trust and believe can manage the financial obligations responsibly.

Communicate with Creditors in Times of Financial Difficulty: If you encounter financial challenges, such as job loss or unexpected medical expenses, reach out to your creditors proactively. Many lenders offer hardship programs or options to modify repayment terms temporarily. This can help you avoid late payments and maintain a positive relationship with your creditors.

Protecting and improving your credit is an ongoing process that requires discipline and vigilance. By consistently monitoring your credit, making timely payments, managing your credit utilization ratio, and adopting responsible credit practices, you can safeguard your credit and enhance your financial well-being.

THE KINGDOM OF HOME BUYING

Securing a home loan involves several steps to ensure a smooth and successful borrowing process. Here are the typical steps involved in obtaining a home loan:

Evaluate Your Financial Readiness: Before applying for a home loan, assess your financial situation. Review your credit report, calculate your debt-to-income ratio, and determine how much you can afford to borrow based on your income, expenses, and down payment savings.

Research and Compare Lenders: Research different lenders, including banks, credit unions, and mortgage companies, to find the best mortgage options. Compare interest rates, loan terms, fees, and customer reviews to identify lenders that suit your needs.

Get Pre-Approved: Obtain a pre-approval letter from your chosen lender. This involves providing necessary documentation such as income verification, bank statements, and credit history. Pre-approval demonstrates to sellers that you are a serious buyer and helps determine your budget for house hunting.

Find a Real Estate Agent: Engage a qualified real estate agent who specializes in your desired location. They will guide you through the home search process, negotiate on your behalf, and assist in ensuring a smooth transaction.

Begin House Hunting: Work with your real estate agent to search for homes that meet your criteria and fall within your budget. Once you find a suitable property, your agent can help you make an offer.

Complete the Loan Application: Once your offer is accepted, you'll need to complete the loan application with your chosen lender. Provide accurate information about the property, your financial situation, employment, income, and assets. The lender will also run a credit check.

Loan Processing and Underwriting: After submitting your application, the lender will start processing your loan. They will verify the information provided, order a home appraisal, and conduct a thorough underwriting process to assess your creditworthiness and the property's value.

Loan Approval and Closing Disclosure: If your loan application is approved, the lender will provide a Closing Disclosure. Review this document carefully, as it outlines the final loan terms, interest rate, closing costs, and any additional requirements.

Arrange Home Inspections and Appraisal: Schedule a professional home inspection to assess the property's condition. Additionally, an appraisal will be conducted to determine the market value of the property. These steps help ensure you are making a sound investment.

Secure Homeowners Insurance: Obtain homeowners insurance coverage for the property, as it is typically a requirement by the lender to protect their investment. Shop around for insurance quotes and provide proof of coverage to the lender.

Finalize Loan Documents: Before the closing, carefully review and sign the loan documents provided by the lender. These documents include the promissory note, deed of trust, and other legal agreements related to the loan.

Closing: Attend the closing meeting, where you'll sign the final paperwork, including the mortgage note, deed, and other relevant documents. You'll also pay closing costs, which typically include lender fees, title fees, prepaid taxes, and insurance.

Funding and Home Ownership: Once all documents are signed and funds are disbursed, you officially become a homeowner. The lender will transfer the loan funds to the seller, and you'll receive the keys to your new home.

Remember, the home loan process can vary based on the lender and your unique circumstances. Stay in close communication with your lender, real estate agent, and other professionals involved to ensure a smooth and successful home buying experience.

THE KINGDOM OF HOME LOANS

When it comes to home loans, there are several types available to suit different borrower needs and circumstances. Here are some of the most common types of home loans and the requirements associated with each:

Conventional Loans:
Conventional loans are not backed by the government and are offered by private lenders. The requirements for conventional loans can vary depending on the lender, but generally, they include:
Good credit score: A higher credit score (typically 620 or above) is generally required for conventional loans, although some lenders may accept lower scores.

Down payment: A down payment of at least 3% to 20% of the home's purchase price is typically required. The exact amount depends on factors like the borrower's credit score, financial history, and the lender's requirements.

Debt-to-income ratio: Lenders typically prefer a debt-to-income ratio (DTI) of 43% or lower. This means that your monthly debts (including the potential mortgage payment) should not exceed 43% of your gross monthly income.

Documentation: You'll need to provide income and asset documentation, including pay stubs, bank statements, and tax returns, to verify your financial stability and ability to repay the loan.

FHA Loans:

FHA (Federal Housing Administration) loans are insured by the government and are designed to make homeownership more accessible, particularly for first-time buyers. The requirements for FHA loans include:

Credit score: While FHA loans are more lenient regarding credit scores, having a minimum credit score of 500-580 is generally required. A higher credit score may enable you to qualify for a lower down payment.

Down payment: The minimum down payment requirement for an FHA loan is 3.5% of the purchase price.

Mortgage insurance: FHA loans require mortgage insurance premiums (MIP) to be paid upfront and as part of the monthly mortgage payment. This insurance protects the lender in case of default.

Debt-to-income ratio: Lenders typically prefer a DTI ratio of 43% or lower, similar to conventional loans.

Documentation: You'll need to provide the necessary documentation to verify your income, employment, and financial stability.

VA Loans:

VA (Veterans Affairs) loans are available to eligible veterans, active-duty service members, and certain surviving spouses. These loans are guaranteed by the Department of Veterans Affairs and offer favorable terms. The requirements for VA loans include:

VA eligibility: You must meet the eligibility criteria set by the VA, such as having served a certain period of time in the military.

Certificate of Eligibility: You'll need to obtain a Certificate of Eligibility (COE) from the VA to prove your eligibility for the loan.

No down payment: VA loans often allow for 100% financing, meaning no down payment is required.

No mortgage insurance: VA loans do not require private mortgage insurance (PMI).

Credit score and DTI ratio: While the VA does not set specific credit score or DTI ratio requirements, lenders may have their own criteria. Generally, a higher credit score and lower DTI ratio will increase your chances of approval.

USDA Loans:

USDA (United States Department of Agriculture) loans are designed to promote homeownership in rural and suburban areas. The requirements for USDA loans include:

Property location: The property being financed must be located in an eligible rural or suburban area as defined by the USDA.

Income limits: USDA loans have income limits based on the area's median income. Your household income must not exceed the specified limit to qualify.

Credit score: While there is no minimum credit score requirement, lenders typically look for a credit score of 640 or higher.

Down payment: USDA loans offer 100% financing, meaning no down payment is required.

Jumbo Loans:

Jumbo loans are used to finance high-value properties that exceed the conforming loan limits set by Fannie Mae and Freddie Mac. The requirements for jumbo loans include:

Higher credit score: Lenders typically require a higher credit score, often above 700, to qualify for a jumbo loan.

Larger down payment: Jumbo loans often require a larger down payment, typically ranging from 10% to 20% or more of the purchase price.

Debt-to-income ratio: Lenders may have stricter DTI ratio requirements for jumbo loans, typically aiming for a ratio below 43%.

Adjustable-Rate Mortgages (ARMs):

ARMs offer an initial fixed interest rate for a certain period, after which the rate adjusts periodically based on market conditions. The requirements for **ARMs include:**

Credit score: The credit score requirements for ARMs are similar to those for conventional loans.

Down payment: The down payment requirement for ARMs is typically the same as for conventional loans. Ability to manage rate fluctuations: Borrowers must demonstrate the ability to handle potential interest rate adjustments when the fixed-rate period ends. Lenders assess this based on the borrower's financial stability and capacity to absorb higher mortgage payments.

Home Equity Loans and Home Equity Lines of Credit (HELOCs):
Home equity loans and HELOCs allow homeowners to borrow against the equity in their homes. The requirements for these loans include:

Sufficient equity: To qualify for a home equity loan or HELOC, you generally need to have a certain amount of equity built up in your property. Lenders may require an LTV (loan-to-value) ratio of 80% or lower.

Credit score: While requirements may vary, lenders typically look for a credit score of 620 or higher for home equity loans and HELOCs.

Debt-to-income ratio: Lenders assess your ability to repay the loan by evaluating your DTI ratio, which is typically preferred to be below 43%.

FHA 203(k) Loans:
FHA 203(k) loans are designed for purchasing or refinancing a home that requires significant repairs or renovations. The requirements for FHA 203(k) loans include:

Property eligibility: The property being financed must meet the FHA's requirements for condition and habitability.

Credit score and DTI ratio: The credit score and DTI ratio requirements for FHA 203(k) loans are similar to those for regular FHA loans.

Contractor and project approval: The loan requires a detailed proposal from a contractor for the repairs or renovations, and the project must be approved by the lender.

It's important to note that the requirements mentioned above are general guidelines, and individual lenders may have additional or varying criteria. It's advisable to consult with lenders directly to understand their specific requirements and determine the best loan option for your needs.

THE KINGDOM OF HOMEOWNERS TAX BENEFITS

Owning a home can provide several tax benefits and opportunities to offset taxes. Here are some ways in which homeownership can help reduce tax liabilities:

Mortgage Interest Deduction: One of the most significant tax benefits of owning a home is the ability to deduct mortgage interest paid on a primary residence or a second home. Homeowners who itemize their deductions can deduct the interest paid on mortgage loans up to a certain limit. The Tax Cuts and Jobs Act (TCJA) introduced changes to this deduction, capping the eligible mortgage debt at

$750,000 for new loans taken after December 15, 2017 (or $1 million for loans taken before that date).

Property Tax Deduction: Homeowners can also deduct property taxes paid on their primary residence and second homes. Property tax deductions can help reduce taxable income, especially for homeowners residing in areas with high property tax rates. It's important to note that the TCJA introduced a cap on the state and local tax (SALT) deduction, which includes property taxes, limiting the total deduction to $10,000 per year.

Home Equity Loan Interest Deduction: Interest paid on home equity loans or home equity lines of credit (HELOCs) may be tax-deductible, subject to certain limitations. Under the TCJA, the interest deduction on home equity debt is only allowed if the loan proceeds are used to buy, build, or substantially improve the property.

Capital Gains Exclusion: When selling a primary residence, homeowners may qualify for a capital gains exclusion. Under current tax laws, if you've lived in your home as your primary residence for at least two out of the five years preceding the sale, you may exclude up to $250,000 of capital gains if you're single, or up to $500,000 if you're married and filing jointly. This exclusion can significantly reduce or eliminate capital gains taxes on the sale of a home.

Energy-Efficient Home Improvements: Homeowners who make qualifying energy-efficient improvements to their homes, such as installing solar panels, energy-efficient windows, or insulation, may be eligible for tax credits. The Residential Renewable Energy Tax Credit and Nonbusiness Energy Property Tax Credit provide incentives to homeowners who make environmentally friendly upgrades to their properties.

Home Office Deduction: If you use a portion of your home exclusively for business purposes, you may be eligible for a home office deduction. This deduction allows you to deduct a portion of your home-related expenses, such as utilities, insurance, and depreciation, based on the square footage of your home office.

Moving Expense Deduction: Although the TCJA eliminated the moving expense deduction for most taxpayers, it still remains available for members of the military in certain circumstances. Military personnel who relocate due to a permanent change of station may be eligible to deduct qualifying moving expenses.

It's important to note that tax laws and regulations can change, and the availability of deductions and credits may vary based on individual circumstances. Consulting with a qualified tax professional or accountant is recommended to understand the specific tax benefits and implications of homeownership in your situation and to ensure compliance with tax laws.

THE KINGDOM OF TAXES

When it comes to tax advice, it's important to note that everyone's tax situation is unique, and it's recommended to consult with a qualified tax professional or accountant for personalized guidance. However, here are some general tax tips that may be helpful:

Understand Your Tax Obligations: Stay informed about your tax obligations by familiarizing yourself with the tax laws and regulations applicable to your situation. This includes knowing the deadlines for filing your tax returns and paying any taxes owed.

Keep Organized Records: Maintain organized and accurate records of your income, expenses, deductions, and receipts. This will help you claim eligible deductions, accurately report your income, and substantiate any claims in case of an audit.

Maximize Available Deductions and Credits: Take advantage of deductions and credits available to you. Some common deductions include mortgage interest, state and local taxes, charitable contributions, and certain medical expenses. Tax credits, such as the Child Tax Credit or the Earned Income Tax Credit, can also help reduce your tax liability.

Contribute to Retirement Accounts: Contributing to retirement accounts, such as a 401(k) or an Individual Retirement Account (IRA), can provide both tax advantages and long-term financial benefits. Contributions to certain retirement accounts may be tax-deductible or provide tax-free growth.

Consider Tax-Efficient Investments: When investing, consider tax-efficient strategies that can help minimize the tax impact on your investment returns. For example, investing in tax-efficient mutual funds or holding investments for more than a year to qualify for lower long-term capital gains tax rates.

Take Advantage of Health Savings Accounts (HSAs) or Flexible Spending Accounts (FSAs): If eligible, contribute to an HSA or FSA to pay for qualified medical expenses with pre-tax dollars. Contributions to HSAs are tax-deductible, and withdrawals for eligible medical expenses are tax-free.

Plan for Tax Changes and Seek Professional Advice: Stay informed about changes to tax laws that may impact your situation. Tax laws can change from year to year, and understanding how those changes may affect your tax liability can help you plan accordingly. Consider consulting with a tax professional to ensure you are making informed decisions.

Review Your Withholding and Adjust if Necessary: Regularly review your withholding to ensure you're paying the right amount of taxes throughout the year. Adjust your withholding if needed to avoid overpaying or underpaying taxes, which can result in a large tax bill or a significant refund.

Consider the Timing of Income and Deductions: Depending on your financial situation, it may be beneficial to defer income or accelerate deductions. For example, if you anticipate a higher income next year, you might consider deferring a bonus payment until the following year to potentially reduce your tax liability.

Stay Organized and File on Time: Maintain good tax habits throughout the year, such as regularly organizing your financial documents and records. File your tax returns on time to avoid penalties and interest charges.

Remember, these tips are general in nature, and individual circumstances may vary. Seek personalized advice from a qualified tax professional to ensure compliance with tax laws and to optimize your tax situation.

THE KINGDOM OF BUSINESS OWNERSHIP

Starting a business can be an exciting but complex endeavor. Here are some important steps to consider when launching a new business:

Develop a Business Idea and Plan: Identify a business idea that aligns with your skills, passion, and market demand. Conduct market research to assess the viability of your idea and create a comprehensive business plan outlining your goals, target market, products or services, marketing strategies, and financial projections.

Conduct a Feasibility Study: Evaluate the feasibility of your business idea by analyzing factors such as market size, competition, potential risks, and financial viability. This study will help you determine if your idea is viable and make any necessary adjustments before proceeding.

Secure Adequate Funding: Determine how much capital you'll need to start and operate your business. Explore different funding options such as personal savings, loans from financial institutions, angel investors, venture capital, or crowdfunding. Create a detailed financial plan to present to potential investors or lenders.

Choose a Legal Structure: Decide on the legal structure of your business, such as a sole proprietorship, partnership, limited liability company (LLC), or corporation. Each structure has different legal, tax, and liability implications, so consult with a legal professional or accountant to determine the most suitable option for your business.

Register Your Business: Register your business name and obtain any necessary licenses and permits required by your local and state government. Register for an Employer Identification Number (EIN) if you plan to hire employees or open a business bank account.

Set Up Business Operations: Establish your physical or virtual business location, set up necessary equipment, technology systems, and infrastructure. Determine your supply chain and establish relationships with vendors and suppliers. Create operational processes and procedures to streamline your business activities. **Develop a Marketing Strategy:** Craft a comprehensive marketing plan to promote your products or services and attract customers. Identify your target audience, establish your unique selling proposition, and develop strategies for online and offline marketing, advertising, branding, and customer acquisition.

Hire and Build a Team: Assess your staffing needs and recruit skilled professionals who align with your business goals. Develop a hiring process, create job descriptions, and conduct interviews to build a competent and motivated team. Consider outsourcing certain functions or utilizing freelancers or consultants as needed.

Set Up Financial Systems: Establish a bookkeeping system to accurately track your business's financial transactions. Open a business bank account to separate personal and business finances. Consider using accounting software to manage invoicing, expenses, and financial reporting.

Obtain Business Insurance: Protect your business and mitigate potential risks by obtaining appropriate insurance coverage. The types of insurance you may need will depend on the nature of your business and can include general liability insurance, professional liability insurance, property insurance, or workers' compensation insurance.

Launch and Monitor: Once all the necessary preparations are in place, officially launch your business. Continuously monitor and evaluate your progress, make necessary adjustments, and stay informed about industry trends and market changes.

Remember that starting a business requires careful planning, research, and perseverance. Seek guidance from mentors, business advisors, and industry experts to increase your chances of success.

THE KINGDOM OF BUSINESS TAX WRITE-OFFS

Owning a business can provide several opportunities to offset taxes legally. Here are some ways in which businesses can help reduce tax liabilities:

Deductible Business Expenses: Business owners can deduct ordinary and necessary expenses incurred while running their business. These expenses may include rent, utilities, office supplies, advertising costs, employee salaries, insurance premiums, professional fees, and travel expenses. By deducting these expenses, business owners can reduce their taxable income.

Depreciation and Amortization: Businesses that own assets such as buildings, equipment, or vehicles can depreciate the value of these assets over time. Depreciation allows businesses to deduct a portion of the asset's cost each year, reducing taxable income. Additionally, businesses can amortize certain intangible assets, such as patents or copyrights, over their useful lives.

Home Office Deduction: If you operate your business from a home office that meets specific IRS criteria, you may be eligible for a home office deduction. This deduction allows you to allocate a portion of your rent or mortgage, utilities, and other related expenses as a deduction against your business income.

Qualified Business Income (QBI) Deduction: Under the Tax Cuts and Jobs Act (TCJA), certain businesses may qualify for a QBI deduction, also known as the Section 199A deduction. This deduction allows eligible businesses, such as sole proprietorships, partnerships, S corporations, and certain LLCs, to deduct up to 20% of their qualified business income. The QBI deduction can significantly reduce the tax burden for eligible business owners.

Retirement Plans: Business owners can take advantage of various retirement plans, such as Simplified Employee Pension (SEP) IRAs, solo 401(k) plans, or individual 401(k) plans. Contributions made to these retirement plans are tax-deductible, allowing business owners to reduce their taxable income while saving for retirement.

Health Savings Accounts (HSAs): For businesses that offer high-deductible health insurance plans, establishing Health Savings Accounts (HSAs) can provide tax advantages. Contributions made to HSAs are tax-deductible, and withdrawals for qualified medical expenses are tax-free.

Tax Credits: Certain business activities and investments may qualify for tax credits, which directly reduce the tax liability. Examples of tax credits include the Research and Development (R&D) Tax Credit, Work Opportunity Tax Credit (WOTC), and Energy-Efficient Commercial Buildings Tax Deduction. These credits can significantly reduce the tax burden for eligible businesses.

Entity Structure: Choosing the right business entity structure, such as a corporation or an LLC, can have tax implications. For example, forming an S corporation may allow business owners to minimize self-employment taxes by separating income into wages and distributions. Consulting with a tax professional can help determine the most tax-efficient entity structure for your business.

It's important to note that tax laws and regulations are subject to change, so staying up-to-date with current tax codes and consulting with a qualified tax professional is crucial. A tax professional can provide personalized advice based on your specific business circumstances and help you navigate the complexities of the tax code to optimize your tax benefits while ensuring compliance.

THE KINGDOM OF APPRECIATION

Asset appreciation refers to the increase in value of an asset over time. It is a key concept in investing and wealth creation, as it allows individuals and businesses to grow their financial resources. In this article, we will delve into the meaning of asset appreciation, explore the factors that drive it, and understand its significance in building long-term prosperity.

Definition and Types of Assets: Asset appreciation pertains to the rise in value of various types of assets. Assets can include real estate, stocks, bonds, precious metals, collectibles, and business ownership, among others. When the value of these assets appreciates, their market price exceeds their initial purchase or acquisition price, resulting in capital gains for the investor.

Factors Driving Asset Appreciation:
Several factors contribute to asset appreciation:

a) Supply and Demand: The basic economic principle of supply and demand plays a significant role in asset appreciation. When the demand for a particular asset exceeds the available supply, its price tends to rise.

b) Economic Conditions: Macroeconomic factors, such as economic growth, inflation rates, interest rates, and government policies, can influence asset values. A robust economy and low inflation often contribute to asset appreciation.

c) Company Performance: In the case of stocks and business ownership, the performance and profitability of the underlying company directly impact asset appreciation. Positive financial results, expansion plans, and innovation tend to drive stock prices higher.

d) Market Sentiment: Investor sentiment and market psychology can greatly influence asset prices. Positive market sentiment, driven by optimism and confidence, can lead to increased demand and asset appreciation.

Importance of Asset Appreciation
Asset appreciation holds several crucial benefits:

a) Wealth Accumulation: Asset appreciation allows individuals and businesses to grow their wealth over time. By investing in appreciating assets, investors can generate capital gains and increase their net worth.

b) Retirement Planning: Asset appreciation plays a vital role in retirement planning. By investing in assets that appreciate consistently, individuals can build a retirement nest egg and secure their financial future.

c) Financial Freedom: Asset appreciation can provide financial freedom by creating additional income streams. Rental properties, for example, can appreciate in value while generating rental income for the owner.

d) Portfolio Diversification: Investing in a range of assets that have the potential for appreciation helps diversify investment portfolios. Diversification mitigates risk and increases the likelihood of overall portfolio growth.

e) Long-Term Prosperity: Asset appreciation, when combined with prudent investment strategies, allows for long-term wealth creation. By holding appreciating assets over an extended period, investors can realize substantial gains and achieve financial prosperity.

Risks and Considerations
While asset appreciation offers the potential for significant returns, it is important to acknowledge the associated risks and exercise caution:

a) Volatility: Asset values can be subject to market fluctuations and volatility. Prices can rise and fall, potentially affecting the overall value of the investment.

b) Market Timing: Timing the market and identifying the right entry and exit points for investments can be challenging. Attempting to time the market can result in missed opportunities or purchasing assets at inflated prices.

c) Investment Research: Conducting thorough research and analysis before investing in assets is essential. Understanding the underlying factors that drive asset appreciation and evaluating the risks involved can contribute to informed investment decisions.

Asset appreciation is a fundamental concept in investment and wealth creation. It signifies the increase in value of various assets over time, providing individuals and businesses with opportunities for growth and financial prosperity. By understanding the factors that drive asset appreciation and considering the associated risks, investors can make informed decisions and harness the power of asset appreciation to build long-term wealth and achieve their financial goals.

THE 3RD JEWEL:
STRATEGIC EDUCATION

Education is a process of acquiring knowledge, skills, values, and attitudes through various forms of learning. It involves the systematic and organized transfer of information and experiences from teachers, instructors, or educational institutions to learners. Education encompasses formal education provided by schools, colleges, and universities, as well as informal learning that occurs through personal experiences, interactions, and self-study.

Education plays a crucial role in personal development, intellectual growth, and the advancement of societies. It equips individuals with the necessary tools and competencies to navigate the world, pursue their goals, and contribute to the betterment of society. Education can take many forms, including academic subjects, practical skills, social and emotional development, and the acquisition of ethical values.

Through education, individuals gain knowledge about various subjects, including mathematics, science, literature, history, and more. It fosters critical thinking, problem-solving, and analytical skills, enabling individuals to make informed decisions and engage in intellectual discourse. Education also promotes creativity, curiosity, and a lifelong love for learning.

Furthermore, education helps individuals develop social skills and emotional intelligence, fostering empathy, teamwork, and effective communication. It promotes cultural understanding, tolerance, and respect for diversity, fostering a sense of global citizenship. Education also plays a vital role in shaping ethical values and moral principles, instilling principles of honesty, integrity, and responsible citizenship.

Education is not limited to a specific age group or formal settings. It is a continuous process that occurs throughout one's life, allowing individuals to adapt to societal changes, technological advancements, and new knowledge. Lifelong learning encourages personal growth, career development, and the ability to adapt to an ever-evolving world. In summary, education is a multifaceted process that empowers individuals with knowledge, skills, values, and attitudes necessary for personal, intellectual, and social growth. It is a lifelong journey that facilitates personal development, equips individuals to face challenges, and contributes to the progress of individuals and society as a whole. Here I will elaborate on building a smart kingdom:

THE KINGDOM OF KNOWLEDGE

What is Strategic Education: To be more strategic in gaining education, consider the following approaches to propel you:

Set Clear Goals: Define your educational goals and objectives. Determine what knowledge, skills, or qualifications you want to acquire. Setting specific, measurable, achievable, relevant, and time-bound (SMART) goals will help you stay focused and motivated.

Conduct a Skills Assessment: Assess your current skills, strengths, and areas for improvement. Identify the skills and knowledge gaps that need to be addressed. This self-reflection will guide you in selecting the right educational opportunities.

Research and Explore Options: Conduct thorough research on available educational options. Consider traditional avenues such as universities, colleges, and vocational schools, as well as online courses, workshops, seminars, and professional development programs. Look for reputable institutions or platforms that offer courses aligned with your goals.

Develop a Learning Plan: Once you have identified your goals and educational options, develop a learning plan. Create a roadmap that outlines the courses, resources, and timelines for your educational journey. Break down larger goals into smaller, actionable steps to make progress.

Prioritize and Focus: With a vast array of educational opportunities, it's essential to prioritize and focus on the areas most relevant to your goals. Identify the core knowledge or skills you need to acquire and prioritize them in your learning plan. This will help you avoid overwhelm and make efficient use of your time and resources.

Seek Diverse Learning Experiences: Expand your educational horizons by seeking diverse learning experiences. Explore different subjects, disciplines, or areas of interest to broaden your knowledge base. Consider interdisciplinary studies that combine multiple fields to gain a holistic understanding.

Network and Collaborate: Engage with fellow learners, instructors, and professionals in your field of interest. Join relevant communities, attend conferences, or participate in online forums. Networking and collaboration can provide valuable insights, support, and opportunities for further learning and growth.

Embrace Continuous Learning: Education doesn't end with formal degrees or certifications. Embrace a mindset of continuous learning. Stay curious, seek new information, and stay updated on the latest trends and developments in your field. Engage in self-study, read books, listen to podcasts, and explore online resources.

Apply Knowledge in Practical Settings: Look for opportunities to apply your acquired knowledge and skills in practical settings. Seek internships, volunteer work, or projects that allow you to gain hands-on experience. Applying what you learn in real-life situations enhances understanding and retention.

Reflect and Evaluate: Regularly reflect on your educational journey. Evaluate your progress, strengths, and areas for improvement. Adjust your learning plan as needed and celebrate milestones and achievements along the way. By adopting a strategic approach to education, you can maximize the value and impact of your learning experiences, making them more aligned with your goals and aspirations. Remember that education is a lifelong process, and each step you take contributes to your personal and professional growth.

THE KINGDOM OF FREE EDUCATION

Sources of Free Education: There are several clever ways to access free education or reduce educational expenses. Here are some strategies you can consider:

Scholarships and Grants: Research and apply for scholarships and grants available from various organizations, institutions, and foundations. Many scholarships are merit-based, while others are need-based or targeted towards specific fields of study. Look for opportunities that align with your background, interests, or goals.

MOOCs and Online Courses: Massive Open Online Courses (MOOCs) offer free or low-cost online courses from renowned universities and institutions. Platforms like Coursera, edX, and Khan Academy provide access to a wide range of subjects taught by experts. While certificates of completion may have a fee, you can often access course materials for free.

Open Educational Resources (OER): OER are freely available educational materials, including textbooks, lectures, and multimedia resources. Platforms like OpenStax, MIT OpenCourseWare, and OpenLearn offer a vast collection of OER across various disciplines. Utilizing these resources can significantly reduce textbook and course material costs.

Community Education Programs: Check if your community, local library, or civic organizations offer free or low-cost educational programs. They may provide workshops, classes, or seminars on a range of topics, allowing you to learn from local experts and engage with the community.

Apprenticeships and Internships: Explore apprenticeship programs or internships that offer on-the-job training and education. Some employers provide educational benefits or cover tuition fees for employees who commit to working with them for a specific period. This can provide valuable learning experiences while gaining practical skills.

Work-Study Programs: If you're pursuing higher education, consider work-study programs offered by colleges and universities. These programs provide part-time employment opportunities on campus, allowing you to earn money while offsetting educational expenses.

Library Resources: Public libraries often provide access to a wealth of educational resources, including books, e-books, audiobooks, research databases, and online learning platforms. Take advantage of these resources to expand your knowledge and skills.

Join Study Groups or Peer Learning Communities: Form or join study groups with like-minded individuals who are interested in similar subjects. Collaborative learning can help you exchange knowledge, share resources, and gain different perspectives. This informal approach can complement your formal education or self-study efforts.

Educational YouTube Channels and Podcasts: Many educators and experts share their knowledge and insights on platforms like YouTube and podcasts. Search for educational channels or podcasts in your areas of interest to access free educational content on a wide range of topics.

Utilize Free Trials and Samples: Some educational platforms or courses offer free trials or samples of their content. Take advantage of these opportunities to explore the quality and relevance of the material before committing to a paid subscription or course. Remember that while these strategies can help you access free or affordable education, they may not replace formal degrees or certifications in certain fields. Consider your specific learning objectives and evaluate the credibility and applicability of the resources or programs you choose.

TECHNICAL SCHOOLS

Technical Schools Versus Colleges: Technical schools, also known as trade schools, and colleges both offer valuable educational pathways, but they differ in their focus and the skills they develop. The value of technical schools versus college depends on individual goals, career aspirations, and personal preferences. Here are some considerations for each:

Practical Skills: Technical schools specialize in providing hands-on training and practical skills in specific trades or industries. They often offer programs that focus on practical applications and job-specific training, such as automotive repair, culinary arts, plumbing, or computer programming. These programs typically have a shorter duration than college programs, allowing students to enter the workforce quickly with the skills needed for a specific career.

Job Market Demand: Technical schools often align their programs with industries experiencing high demand for skilled workers. This means graduates may have more immediate job opportunities and potentially higher earning potential in fields where there is a shortage of skilled professionals.

Cost and Time Investment: Trade schools generally have lower tuition fees and shorter program durations compared to colleges. This can make technical education more affordable and appealing for individuals who want to enter the workforce sooner without incurring significant student debt. Additionally, shorter program lengths mean students can start earning income sooner.

Flexibility and Specialization: Technical schools offer specialized programs tailored to specific careers or industries. This focus allows students to acquire in-depth knowledge and skills in a particular area, making them more competitive in their chosen field. It can also provide greater flexibility for individuals who have a clear career path in mind and want to pursue targeted training.

Transferability of Credits: While technical school credits may not always transfer directly to colleges or universities, some institutions have articulation agreements in place that allow technical school graduates to receive credits toward a college degree. This can provide a pathway for individuals who wish to further their education and earn a higher degree in the future.

Liberal Arts Education: Colleges often provide a broader education through a liberal arts curriculum. They offer a wide range of academic disciplines, allowing students to explore diverse subjects and develop critical thinking, communication, and research skills. A college degree is typically required for careers that demand advanced knowledge or positions in certain industries, such as engineering, healthcare, or academia.

Career Advancement Opportunities: While technical school programs may lead directly to entry-level positions, college degrees can provide broader career opportunities and a foundation for long-term professional growth. Some careers require higher education credentials, and colleges often offer graduate programs for individuals seeking specialized knowledge or leadership roles.

Ultimately, the value of technical schools versus college depends on your career goals, learning style, financial situation, and the specific industry you wish to enter. It can be helpful to research the requirements and expectations of your desired field to determine which educational path aligns best with your aspirations. Additionally, consider seeking guidance from professionals in your chosen industry or academic advisors who can provide insights based on their expertise and experience.

THE KINGDOM OF CERTIFICATION

Certifications Versus Degrees: Both certifications and college degrees can be valuable in different ways, depending on the industry, career goals, and individual circumstances. Here's an overview of their respective benefits:

CERTIFICATIONS

Targeted Skills: Certifications focus on specific skills and knowledge required for a particular job or industry. They provide a concentrated and practical education that can make you job-ready in a shorter timeframe compared to a broader college degree.

Industry Recognition: Certifications are often recognized and respected within specific industries. They demonstrate to employers that you possess the necessary skills and expertise in a particular field, enhancing your credibility and employability.

Career Advancement: Certifications can open doors for career advancement or promotions. They showcase your commitment to professional development and continuous learning, which can help you stand out among peers and qualify for higher-level positions.

Cost and Time Investment: Certifications are generally more affordable and time-efficient compared to college degrees. They often require less time and financial commitment, making them a more accessible option for individuals seeking to enhance their skills or pivot into a new career without pursuing a full degree.

THE KINGDOM OF COLLEGE

COLLEGE DEGREES

Broader Knowledge Base: College degrees provide a broader education across various subjects, offering a well-rounded understanding of the world and developing critical thinking, analytical, and communication skills. They can foster intellectual growth and provide a foundation for lifelong learning.

Career Opportunities: Certain careers and industries require a college degree as a minimum qualification. Degrees can provide access to a wider range of job opportunities and industries that prioritize higher education credentials, such as engineering, healthcare, education, and research.

Networking and Resources: Colleges offer extensive networking opportunities, connections with industry professionals, and access to resources like libraries, research facilities, and internships. These resources can contribute to personal and professional growth and provide a supportive environment for learning and career development.

Personal Development: College experiences often involve personal growth, independence, and the development of soft skills like teamwork, time management, and problem-solving. The holistic nature of a college education can shape well-rounded individuals with a broader perspective.

It's important to note that the value of certifications and college degrees may vary by industry and specific job requirements. Some industries may prioritize certifications as a measure of competency, while others may place greater emphasis on formal degrees. In certain cases, a combination of both certifications and a college degree may be ideal for maximizing career prospects and professional growth.

Ultimately, the choice between certifications and college degrees depends on your career goals, industry requirements, and personal circumstances. Consider researching the specific job market and seeking advice from professionals in your desired field to determine the most suitable educational path for your aspirations.

NON-DEGREE CAREERS

NO-DEGREE REQUIRED, HIGH-PAYING CAREERS: There are several high-paying career fields that don't necessarily require a traditional college degree. While some of these careers may require alternative forms of education, certifications, or extensive experience, they offer opportunities for individuals to enter well-compensated professions. Here are a few examples:

Information Technology (IT): Positions in IT, such as computer programming, web development, cybersecurity, and network administration, often prioritize technical skills and certifications over formal degrees. Professionals in these fields can earn competitive salaries based on their expertise and experience.

Trades and Skilled Labor: Careers in skilled trades, such as electricians, plumbers, HVAC technicians, carpenters, and welders, can be financially rewarding. Apprenticeships, vocational training programs, and relevant certifications are typically required for these roles.

Sales and Business Development: Sales professionals, especially those in high-demand sectors like software sales, pharmaceutical sales, or real estate, can earn substantial incomes through commissions and bonuses. While a degree may not be required, strong communication, negotiation, and relationship-building skills are essential.

Commercial Piloting: Becoming a commercial pilot can lead to well-paying opportunities, particularly in the airline industry. Pilots acquire their licenses through flight schools, which offer structured training programs.

Entrepreneurship and Small Business Ownership: Starting your own business or becoming an entrepreneur in a lucrative industry can yield significant financial rewards. Success often depends on personal drive, business acumen, and industry-specific knowledge.

Real Estate: Real estate agents, brokers, and property managers can earn high incomes through commissions and fees. While a degree is not mandatory, acquiring relevant licenses, certifications, and market knowledge is crucial.

Digital Marketing and Social Media Management: In the digital age, expertise in online marketing, search engine optimization, social media management, and content creation can lead to well-paying positions. Building a portfolio, gaining relevant certifications, and demonstrating results are key to success in this field.

Creative Arts and Entertainment: Careers in the creative arts, such as photography, graphic design, music production, or acting, can be financially rewarding for talented individuals who can establish themselves in the industry without a formal degree.

It's important to note that while a college degree may not be a prerequisite for these careers, acquiring specialized skills, certifications, or relevant industry experience is often necessary. Additionally, the earning potential may vary based on factors such as location, industry demand, and individual expertise.

It's advisable to thoroughly research and understand the requirements, career paths, and market conditions of your desired field to determine the most appropriate educational and skill-building pathways for achieving financial success.

THE KINGDOM OF ONLINE INCOME

Making Money Online: Making money online offers a range of opportunities for individuals seeking flexibility, independence, and the potential for financial growth. Here are several ways to make money online:

Freelancing: Offer your skills and services as a freelancer. Platforms like Upwork, Freelancer, and Fiverr connect freelancers with clients seeking various services such as writing, graphic design, programming, virtual assistance, and more. Build a portfolio, establish your expertise, and market your services to attract clients.

E-commerce and Online Retail: Create an online store to sell products. Platforms like Shopify, WooCommerce, and Etsy enable you to set up an online storefront easily. You can sell physical products, digital goods, or even dropship products from suppliers. Develop a niche, source or create products, and utilize effective marketing strategies to drive sales.

Online Consulting or Coaching: If you have expertise in a specific field, offer consulting or coaching services online. Whether it's business, career, fitness, nutrition, or personal development, people are often willing to pay for expert guidance and advice. Establish your credibility, create tailored programs or services, and market yourself through social media, content creation, and networking.

Online Teaching and Tutoring: Utilize your knowledge and skills to teach others online. Platforms like Udemy and Teachable allow you to create and sell online courses. Additionally, you can offer tutoring or language lessons through platforms like VIPKid or iTalki. Prepare engaging content, demonstrate expertise, and market your courses or tutoring services to reach your target audience.

Content Creation: Monetize your creativity and knowledge through content creation. Start a blog, YouTube channel, or podcast where you provide valuable information, entertainment, or insights. As your audience grows, you can generate income through advertising, sponsorships, affiliate marketing, or creating and selling digital products.

Online Surveys and Microtasks: Participate in online surveys or complete microtasks on platforms like Amazon Mechanical Turk or Swagbucks. While the payouts for individual tasks may be small, they can add up over time, providing some supplemental income.

Affiliate Marketing: Promote products or services through affiliate marketing. You earn a commission for each sale or lead generated through your referral. Join affiliate programs related to your niche or industry and promote products through your website, blog, social media, or email marketing.

Stock Trading or Investing: Engage in online stock trading or investing in financial markets. Platforms like Robinhood, eToro, or TD Ameritrade offer accessible ways to buy and sell stocks, cryptocurrencies, or other financial instruments. However, note that trading and investing involve risks, and thorough research and understanding are essential.

Online Surplus Sales: Sell items you no longer need through online marketplaces like eBay, Facebook Marketplace, or Craigslist. Utilize your skills in negotiating, marketing, and customer service to maximize your profits.

Online Surveys and User Testing: Participate in market research studies, surveys, or user testing for companies and organizations. Platforms like UserTesting and Survey Junkie offer opportunities to provide feedback and insights, earning money for your time and opinions. When pursuing online money-making opportunities, keep in mind that success often requires dedication, consistency, and adapting to changing trends and market demands. Select a method that aligns with your skills, interests, and long-term goals, and be prepared to invest time and effort into building your online presence and reputation.

Build & Monetize Social Media Followings: Building a large social media following and monetizing it can be a rewarding venture. While success varies based on individual circumstances and platforms, here are some strategies to consider:

Choose the Right Platform: Select the social media platform that aligns with your content and target audience. Each platform has its own characteristics and demographics. For visual content, consider Instagram or Pinterest. For video content, explore YouTube or TikTok. For professional networking, LinkedIn may be suitable.

Define Your Niche: Identify your area of expertise or passion and focus your content around it. Having a clear niche helps attract a specific audience interested in your content. This targeted audience is more likely to engage with your posts and become loyal followers.

Consistent and Quality Content: Regularly post high-quality content that adds value to your followers. Develop a content strategy that aligns with your niche and provides information, entertainment, inspiration, or education. Engage with your audience by responding to comments and messages promptly.

Use Engaging Visuals: Visuals play a crucial role in attracting attention on social media. Invest in creating visually appealing content such as captivating images, videos, infographics, or animations. Use relevant hashtags to increase discoverability.

Build Authentic Relationships: Interact with your audience by responding to comments, initiating conversations, and participating in relevant discussions. Show genuine interest in your followers, and foster a sense of community by creating opportunities for them to engage with each other.

Collaborate with Others: Collaborate with influencers, content creators, or brands in your niche. Collaborations can expose your content to a wider audience and help you gain followers. Consider guest posting, participating in joint ventures, or cross-promoting each other's content.

Engage with Influencers and Brands: Engage with influential figures and brands in your niche by commenting, sharing, and mentioning them in your posts. This can increase your visibility and attract their followers to your profile. Additionally, consider sponsored collaborations or brand partnerships to monetize your following.

Utilize Analytics and Insights: Pay attention to the analytics and insights provided by social media platforms. Understand your audience demographics, engagement rates, and popular content types. This data can guide your content strategy and help you optimize your approach.

Monetization Strategies: There are various ways to monetize a large social media following:

Brand Partnerships: Collaborate with brands for sponsored posts, endorsements, or ambassadorships.

Affiliate Marketing: Promote products or services and earn a commission for each sale generated through your referral.

Digital Products: Create and sell digital products like e-books, online courses, or digital artwork.

Advertising: Utilize platforms that offer advertising options, such as YouTube's Partner Program or Instagram's IGTV Ads.

Sponsored Content: Get paid to feature or review products, services, or events on your social media channels. Remember, building a substantial following takes time, effort, and consistency. Focus on creating valuable content, engaging with your audience, and adapting to the evolving social media landscape. Stay authentic, stay true to your brand, and consistently explore opportunities to monetize your following while providing value to your audience.

THE 4ᵀᴴ JEWEL: HEALTHY LIVING

Healthy living is a holistic approach to maintaining and improving one's overall well-being. It encompasses various aspects of physical, mental, and emotional health. Here's a detailed explanation of the importance of healthy living towards building a lasting kingdom:

Physical Health: Engaging in healthy habits promotes physical well-being, which is crucial for overall quality of life. Regular exercise, balanced nutrition, and adequate sleep are fundamental components of physical health. Benefits include:

Disease Prevention: Adopting a healthy lifestyle can reduce the risk of chronic diseases such as heart disease, diabetes, obesity, and certain types of cancer.

Increased Energy and Vitality: Regular physical activity and a nutritious diet enhance energy levels, stamina, and overall vitality, allowing you to fully participate in daily activities.

Strong Immune System: A healthy lifestyle supports a robust immune system, making you less susceptible to infections and illnesses.

Improved Physical Function: Exercise helps maintain muscle strength, flexibility, and bone density, improving mobility and reducing the risk of falls and injuries.

Mental and Emotional Well-being: Healthy living positively impacts mental and emotional health, contributing to a more balanced and fulfilling life.

Key Benefits Include:

Reduced Stress and Anxiety: Regular exercise, stress management techniques, and self-care practices can alleviate stress, reduce anxiety, and improve overall mental well-being.

Enhanced Mood and Emotional Resilience: Engaging in healthy habits, such as exercise, adequate sleep, and a balanced diet, releases endorphins and neurotransmitters that improve mood and promote emotional resilience.

Better Cognitive Function: A healthy lifestyle, including proper nutrition and regular physical activity, supports optimal brain function, memory, focus, and cognitive abilities.

Improved Sleep Quality: Prioritizing healthy living habits can contribute to better sleep quality, which is crucial for mental and emotional restoration, concentration, and emotional stability.

Longevity and Quality of Life: Adopting a healthy lifestyle has a significant impact on longevity and overall quality of life. It enables you to enjoy life to the fullest, maintain independence, and engage in activities that bring joy and fulfillment.

Increased Lifespan: Healthy living practices, such as maintaining a healthy weight, regular physical activity, and a balanced diet, have been linked to longer lifespans.

Prevention of Age-Related Health Issues: A healthy lifestyle can help prevent or delay age-related health conditions, improving quality of life and reducing healthcare costs.

Improved Mental Function in Later Years: Engaging in healthy habits throughout life can contribute to better cognitive function and memory retention as you age.

Greater Resilience to Health Challenges: Healthy living practices strengthen the body's resilience and ability to recover from illnesses or injuries, ensuring a faster and smoother recovery.

Personal and Professional Success: Healthy living positively impacts personal and professional success by fostering self-confidence, increased productivity, and a positive mindset.

Boosted Self-Confidence: Engaging in healthy habits improves self-esteem and body image, leading to increased self-confidence and a positive self-perception.

Increased Productivity and Focus: A healthy lifestyle supports mental clarity, concentration, and productivity, enabling you to perform better in personal and professional endeavors.

Positive Mindset and Emotional Resilience: Healthy living practices contribute to a positive mindset, emotional resilience, and the ability to handle challenges effectively, leading to personal and professional growth. In summary, embracing a healthy lifestyle is essential for achieving and maintaining optimal physical, mental, and emotional well-being. It promotes longevity, reduces the risk of chronic diseases, enhances quality of life, and contributes to personal and professional success. By prioritizing healthy living, you empower yourself to lead a fulfilling, balanced, and vibrant life.

THE KINGDOM OF EXERCISE

Improving Your Physical Health: Improving physical health involves adopting healthy habits and making positive lifestyle changes. Here are detailed strategies to enhance physical well-being:

Regular Exercise:
Choose Activities You Enjoy: Engage in physical activities that you find enjoyable and suit your fitness

level. This can include walking, jogging, swimming, cycling, dancing, or participating in team sports.

Set Realistic Goals: Start with achievable goals and gradually increase the intensity and duration of your workouts. This helps prevent injuries and keeps you motivated.

Incorporate Strength Training: Include strength training exercises at least twice a week to build muscle strength, improve bone density, and support overall physical function.

Stay Active Throughout the Day: Incorporate movement into your daily routine by taking regular breaks from sitting, using stairs instead of elevators, or walking or biking for short errands.

Incorporating Exercise Into Your Daily Life: Incorporating physical activity into your daily life is an excellent way to make it a consistent and sustainable part of your routine. Here are some practical tips to help you seamlessly integrate physical activity into your daily living:

Set Realistic Goals: Start by setting realistic and achievable goals for physical activity. Aim to engage in at least 150 minutes of moderate-intensity aerobic activity or 75 minutes of vigorous-intensity aerobic activity each week, as recommended by health authorities. Break it down into smaller chunks of time throughout the day if needed.

Find Activities You Enjoy: Choose physical activities that you genuinely enjoy. This increases the likelihood of sticking with them in the long run. It could be walking, jogging, dancing, cycling, swimming, playing a sport, or even gardening. Experiment with different activities to find what suits your interests and fits well with your lifestyle.

Schedule Exercise: Treat physical activity as an essential appointment in your daily schedule. Set aside dedicated time for exercise and make it a priority. Consider blocking off time on your calendar or incorporating it into your morning or evening routine.

Active Commuting: Whenever possible, choose active modes of transportation such as walking or cycling instead of driving or taking public transport. If the distance is too far, consider parking your vehicle farther away from your destination and walking the rest of the way.

Breaks and Movement: Take short breaks throughout the day to move and stretch. If you have a sedentary job, stand up and stretch every hour, or consider using a standing desk or stability ball. Take short walks during your lunch break or use stairs instead of elevators whenever feasible.

Household Chores: Engage in household activities that involve physical movement. Cleaning, gardening, vacuuming, mowing the lawn, or washing the car are all activities that can contribute to your daily physical activity.

Active Socializing: Plan active social activities with friends and family. Instead of meeting for coffee or meals, consider going for a hike, playing a game, or participating in a group fitness class together.

Make It a Family Affair: Encourage your family members to engage in physical activities together. This could include taking walks after dinner, playing outdoor games, or going on weekend bike rides.

Use Technology: Utilize fitness apps, fitness trackers, or smartwatches to monitor your activity levels, set goals, and track progress. These tools can provide motivation and help you stay accountable.

Stay Flexible: Be flexible with your exercise routine. If you miss a planned workout or don't have time for a full session, find opportunities for physical activity throughout the day. Even short bursts of activity, like taking the stairs or doing a quick workout video, can add up and make a difference. Remember, it's important to listen to your body, start gradually, and gradually increase the intensity and duration of your physical activity. By incorporating exercise into your daily living, you'll reap the benefits of improved fitness, better overall health, and enhanced well-being.

Good Workout Routine: A well-rounded exercise routine that combines strength training and cardiovascular exercises can help you build strength and improve heart health. Here's a sample exercise routine that targets both aspects:

Warm-Up: Begin with 5-10 minutes of light cardiovascular activity such as brisk walking, cycling, or jumping jacks to increase your heart rate and warm up your muscles. Follow it with dynamic stretches to mobilize your joints and prepare your body for the workout.

Strength Training: Perform strength training exercises 2-3 times per week, targeting major muscle groups. Aim for 8-12 repetitions of each exercise, completing 2-3 sets with a brief rest period between sets. Include exercises such as squats, lunges, push-ups, chest presses, rows, shoulder presses, bicep curls, tricep dips, and core exercises like planks or crunches. Progressively increase the weight or resistance used as you become stronger to continue challenging your muscles.

Cardiovascular Exercise: Engage in moderate-intensity cardiovascular exercises on most days of the week, aiming for a total of 150 minutes or more per week. This can be broken down into shorter sessions of 30 minutes or more. Options include brisk walking, jogging, cycling, swimming, dancing, or using cardio machines like treadmills, ellipticals, or stationary bikes. Incorporate interval training, alternating between periods of higher intensity (e.g., faster pace or higher resistance) and recovery periods of lower intensity. Gradually increase the duration and intensity of your cardiovascular workouts as your fitness improves.

Flexibility and Mobility: Include stretching exercises to improve flexibility and mobility. Stretch major muscle groups after each workout or dedicate separate sessions to stretching and mobility exercises. Hold each stretch for 15-30 seconds and perform stretches for all major muscle groups, including legs, hips, back, chest, shoulders, and arms. Consider activities like yoga or Pilates, which combine strength, flexibility, and balance.

Cool-Down: Finish each workout session with a 5-10 minute cool-down period, gradually reducing the intensity of your activity. This helps your heart rate and breathing to return to normal gradually. Conclude with static stretches, holding each stretch for 15-30 seconds to promote muscle recovery and flexibility.

Rest and Recovery: Allow for rest days between strength training sessions to give your muscles time to repair and grow stronger. Listen to your body and modify your routine as needed to prevent overexertion or injury. Remember, it's essential to consult with a healthcare professional or a certified fitness trainer before starting any new exercise program, especially if you have any underlying health conditions or concerns. They can provide personalized guidance based on your specific needs and help you progress safely.

THE KINGDOM OF NUTRITION

Incorporating Healthier Eating: Incorporating a healthier and more nutritious diet involves making conscious choices about the foods you consume and adopting sustainable eating habits. Here are detailed strategies to help you incorporate a nutritious diet:

Eat a Variety of Nutrient-Dense Foods
Include Fruits and Vegetables: Aim to fill half your plate with a colorful assortment of fruits and vegetables. These provide essential vitamins, minerals, fiber, and antioxidants.

Choose Whole Grains: Opt for whole grains such as brown rice, quinoa, whole wheat bread, and oatmeal, which offer more fiber, nutrients, and sustained energy compared to refined grains.

Include Lean Proteins: Incorporate lean sources of protein like skinless poultry, fish, tofu, legumes, and low-fat dairy products. These are rich in amino acids, vitamins, and minerals.

Healthy Fats: Include sources of healthy fats like avocados, nuts, seeds, olive oil, and fatty fish. These provide essential fatty acids and help support heart health.

Dairy or Dairy Alternatives: Choose low-fat or fat-free dairy products or suitable alternatives like almond milk or soy milk for calcium and other nutrients.

Portion Control and Mindful Eating: Be mindful of portion sizes and avoid oversized servings. Use smaller plates and bowls to help control portion sizes and eat until you are satisfied, not overly full. Practice mindful eating by paying attention to your hunger and fullness cues. Eat slowly, savor the flavors, and listen to your body's signals of satiety.

Limit Added Sugars and Processed Foods
Minimize Sugary Drinks: Cut back on sugary beverages like soda, sports drinks, and sweetened juices. Choose water, herbal tea, or unsweetened alternatives instead.

Reduce Added Sugars: Read food labels and be aware of hidden sugars in processed foods like cereals, sauces, condiments, and snacks. Opt for naturally sweetened options or make your own meals and snacks using whole ingredients.

Minimize Processed Foods: Limit your intake of highly processed foods that are often high in unhealthy fats, sodium, and additives. Opt for whole, unprocessed foods as much as possible.

Meal Planning and Preparation: Plan your meals and snacks ahead of time to ensure you have nutritious options readily available. This helps avoid relying on unhealthy convenience foods. Prepare meals at home as often as possible, where you have control over the ingredients and cooking methods used. Batch cook and meal prep on weekends or your days off to save time during busy weekdays. Preparing larger portions allows for leftovers that can be used for future meals.

Hydration and Beverage Choices: Drink an adequate amount of water throughout the day to stay hydrated. Water supports various bodily functions and helps regulate appetite.

Limit or avoid sugary beverages, high-calorie coffee drinks, and alcohol. These can add unnecessary calories and may have adverse effects on health.

Read and Understand Food Labels: Learn to read food labels and understand the nutritional information. Look for ingredients lists and choose foods with fewer additives, artificial sweeteners, and preservatives. Pay attention to serving sizes, calorie content, and nutrient breakdowns to make informed choices about the foods you consume.

Seek Professional Guidance: Consult a registered dietitian or nutritionist for personalized guidance, especially if you have specific dietary needs, health concerns, or weight management goals. They can help create a customized meal plan, provide nutritional recommendations, and support you in making sustainable dietary changes. Remember, adopting a healthier and more nutritious diet is a gradual process. Focus on making small, sustainable changes over time, rather than aiming for perfection.

Balanced Nutrition

Eat a Varied Diet: Consume a wide variety of nutrient-dense foods, including fruits, vegetables, whole grains, lean proteins, and healthy fats. Aim for a balanced mix of macronutrients (carbohydrates, proteins, and fats) and micronutrients (vitamins and minerals).

Portion Control: Be mindful of portion sizes and avoid overeating. Practice portion control by using smaller plates, measuring servings, and listening to your body's hunger and fullness cues.

Hydration: Drink an adequate amount of water throughout the day to stay hydrated. Limit the consumption of sugary drinks and opt for water, herbal tea, or infused water instead.

Minimize Processed Foods: Reduce the intake of highly processed foods, which are often high in added sugars, unhealthy fats, and artificial additives. Focus on whole, unprocessed foods for optimal nutrition.

THE KINGDOM OF FASTING

Fasting, the practice of voluntarily abstaining from food or drink for a specific period, has been followed for centuries in various cultures and religions. Beyond its spiritual and cultural significance, fasting offers a wide range of benefits for physical and mental health. This article explores the numerous advantages of fasting and sheds light on its potential impact on overall well-being.

Weight Loss and Metabolic Health: One of the primary benefits of fasting is its potential for weight loss. By creating a calorie deficit, fasting can promote fat burning and help reduce excess body weight. Additionally, fasting has been shown to enhance metabolic health by improving insulin sensitivity, reducing inflammation, and optimizing hormone levels, leading to better blood sugar control and a decreased risk of type 2 diabetes.

Cellular Repair and Autophagy: During fasting, the body initiates a cellular repair process called autophagy. This mechanism involves the recycling of damaged cellular components and the removal of accumulated waste products. Autophagy is believed to contribute to longevity, protect against age-related diseases, and support overall cellular health.

Improved Brain Function: Fasting has been shown to have beneficial effects on brain health and cognitive function. Studies suggest that fasting can enhance the production of brain-derived neurotrophic factor (BDNF), a protein that promotes the growth and maintenance of neurons. Increased BDNF levels have been associated with improved memory, focus, and overall brain function.

Reduced Inflammation: Chronic inflammation is linked to various health conditions, including heart disease, cancer, and autoimmune disorders. Fasting has been found to reduce inflammation markers in the body. By suppressing inflammation, fasting may help prevent and manage inflammatory diseases, promoting overall health and well-being.

Enhanced Heart Health: Fasting has been shown to improve several risk factors for heart disease. It can lower blood pressure, reduce LDL cholesterol levels, and decrease triglyceride levels, thus reducing the risk of cardiovascular complications. These benefits contribute to better heart health and a reduced likelihood of heart-related illnesses.

Increased Energy and Mental Clarity: Many individuals report increased energy levels and mental clarity during fasting periods. By allowing the digestive system to rest, fasting redirects energy to other bodily functions, such as cellular repair and metabolic processes. This revitalization can lead to heightened focus, improved productivity, and increased mental alertness.

Emotional Well-being and Stress Reduction: Fasting has the potential to positively impact emotional well-being. It may help regulate mood and alleviate symptoms of depression and anxiety. Additionally, fasting has been found to reduce the production of stress hormones, such as cortisol, thereby promoting relaxation and stress reduction.

Longevity and Anti-Aging Effects: Emerging research suggests that fasting may have anti-aging effects and promote longevity. Caloric restriction, a form of fasting, has been shown to extend lifespan in various organisms. By reducing oxidative stress, promoting cellular repair, and improving metabolic health, fasting may slow down the aging process and increase lifespan.

Detoxification and Cleansing: Fasting allows the body to undergo a natural detoxification process. During fasting, the body utilizes stored fat and mobilizes toxins stored in fat cells, aiding in their elimination. This cleansing effect supports liver function and enhances the body's natural detoxification mechanisms.

Spiritual and Mindful Connection: Fasting has deep-rooted spiritual and mindful associations. It can foster a sense of discipline, self-control, and mindfulness. For many individuals, fasting serves as a period of introspection, self-reflection, and spiritual growth.

Fasting offers a myriad of benefits that encompass physical, mental, and emotional well-being. From weight loss and improved metabolic health to cellular repair and enhanced brain function, fasting has shown scientific evidence of its benefits.

TYPES OF FASTING: There are various types of fasting, each with its unique approach and potential advantages. This comprehensive article aims to provide an overview of the different types of fasting and delve into their specific benefits.

Time-Restricted Feeding (TRF):
Time-restricted feeding involves limiting the daily eating window to a specific period, typically between 8 to 12 hours, while fasting for the remaining

hours. The most common TRF method is the 16:8 approach, where individuals fast for 16 hours and consume all their calories within an 8-hour window. Benefits of TRF include:

Weight Loss: TRF helps create a calorie deficit and promotes weight loss by reducing overall calorie intake.

Improved Metabolic Health: TRF can enhance insulin sensitivity, regulate blood sugar levels, and promote better metabolic function.

Enhanced Cellular Repair: Fasting periods in TRF trigger autophagy, allowing for cellular repair and rejuvenation.

Increased Energy and Mental Clarity: TRF can lead to increased energy levels, improved focus, and mental clarity during the fasting period.

Alternate-Day Fasting (ADF):

Alternate-day fasting involves alternating between fasting days and regular eating days. On fasting days, individuals consume very few calories (typically 500-600 calories) or no food at all. Benefits of ADF include:

Weight Loss: ADF promotes calorie restriction, leading to significant weight loss over time.

Improved Insulin Sensitivity: ADF can enhance insulin sensitivity, potentially reducing the risk of type 2 diabetes.

Enhanced Fat Burning: During fasting days, the body relies on stored fat for energy, promoting fat burning and weight loss.

Potential Longevity Effects: ADF may trigger cellular repair mechanisms and promote longevity through enhanced autophagy.

Extended Fasting: Extended fasting refers to fasting for more extended periods, typically ranging from 24 hours to several days or even weeks. Common approaches include 24-hour fasts, 48-hour fasts, or longer fasts lasting several days. Benefits of extended fasting include:

Deep Cellular Repair: Extended fasting initiates extensive autophagy, allowing for thorough cellular repair and regeneration.

Enhanced Insulin Sensitivity and Fat Burning: Longer fasting periods can lead to improved insulin sensitivity and increased fat burning for energy.

Immune System Rejuvenation: Extended fasting may help reset and regenerate the immune system, promoting overall health and resilience.

Mental Clarity and Spiritual Reflection: Extended fasting can provide mental clarity, promote introspection, and deepen the spiritual experience for some individuals.

Intermittent Fasting (IF): Intermittent fasting is a broad term that encompasses various fasting patterns, including the previously mentioned TRF and ADF. The flexibility of IF allows individuals to choose a fasting approach that suits their lifestyle and preferences. Benefits of intermittent fasting include:

Weight Loss and Improved Body Composition: IF can facilitate weight loss, reduce body fat, and preserve muscle mass.

Enhanced Metabolic Health: IF improves insulin sensitivity, regulates blood sugar levels, and supports overall metabolic function.

Reduced Inflammation: IF has been shown to reduce markers of inflammation in the body, which may contribute to improved health and disease prevention.

Cognitive Function and Brain Health: IF has been associated with improved brain function, increased focus, and enhanced cognitive performance.

INTERMITTENT FASTING:

Intermittent fasting is an eating pattern that involves alternating periods of fasting and eating. Here are some of the key benefits of intermittent fasting:

Weight Loss: Intermittent fasting can help facilitate weight loss by creating a calorie deficit and increasing fat burning. It promotes body fat reduction while preserving muscle mass.

Improved Insulin Sensitivity: Intermittent fasting enhances insulin sensitivity, allowing the body to use insulin more effectively. This can lead to better blood sugar control, reduced risk of type 2 diabetes, and improved overall metabolic health.

Cellular Repair and Autophagy: During fasting, the body initiates autophagy, a cellular repair process that removes damaged cells and promotes cellular renewal. This can contribute to improved longevity and protection against age-related diseases.

Reduced Inflammation: Intermittent fasting has been shown to reduce inflammation in the body, which is associated with various chronic diseases. By suppressing inflammation, it may help alleviate symptoms of conditions like arthritis and improve overall health.

Heart Health: Intermittent fasting can lower blood pressure, reduce LDL cholesterol levels, and decrease triglyceride levels, all of which contribute to better heart health and a reduced risk of cardiovascular diseases.

Cognitive Function: Some studies suggest that intermittent fasting may enhance brain function and improve cognitive abilities. It may boost brain-derived neurotrophic factor (BDNF), a protein that promotes the growth and survival of neurons.

Increased Energy and Focus: Many people experience increased energy levels and improved mental clarity during fasting periods. By allowing the digestive system to rest, fasting redirects energy to other bodily functions, leading to heightened focus and increased productivity.

Convenience and Simplified Eating: Intermittent fasting can simplify meal planning and eating patterns. By restricting the eating window, individuals may find it easier to adhere to a healthy eating regimen and avoid excessive snacking or mindless eating.

Time-Saving: With intermittent fasting, there is often no need to spend time preparing or eating breakfast, allowing individuals to save time in their daily routine.

Flexibility and Adaptability: Intermittent fasting is a flexible approach that can be tailored to individual preferences and lifestyles. It can be adapted to fit different schedules and dietary preferences, making it accessible to a wide range of individuals.

It's important to note that while intermittent fasting offers several potential benefits, it may not be suitable for everyone. It is advisable to consult a healthcare professional before starting any new diet or fasting regimen, especially for individuals with certain medical conditions or specific dietary needs.

THE KINGDOM OF SLEEP

Quality Sleep
Establish a Routine: Set a consistent sleep schedule by going to bed and waking up at the same time each day, even on weekends.

Create a Sleep-friendly Environment: Ensure your sleep environment is cool, dark, quiet, and comfortable. Use blackout curtains, earplugs, white noise machines, or eye masks if needed.

Practice Relaxation Techniques: Wind down before bedtime by engaging in calming activities such as reading, taking a warm bath, practicing meditation or deep breathing exercises.

Limit Stimulants: Avoid consuming caffeine, nicotine, or alcohol close to bedtime, as they can disrupt sleep patterns.

Stress Management
Identify Stressors: Recognize the sources of stress in your life and develop strategies to manage them effectively. This may include time management, setting boundaries, or seeking support from friends, family, or professionals.

Practice Relaxation Techniques: Engage in stress-reducing activities such as yoga, meditation, deep breathing exercises, or mindfulness practices.

Regular Physical Activity: Exercise regularly as it helps reduce stress levels and promotes the release of endorphins, which improve mood and relaxation.

Prioritize Self-Care: Make time for activities that bring you joy and relaxation, whether it's hobbies, spending time in nature, listening to music, or engaging in creative outlets.

THE KINGDOM OF REGULAR CHECKUPS

Regular Health Check-ups/Doctor's Visits

Schedule Routine Check-ups: Regularly visit your healthcare provider for preventive screenings, vaccinations, and general health assessments.

Know Your Numbers: Keep track of your vital health indicators such as blood pressure, cholesterol levels, and body mass index (BMI). Understanding your numbers helps you make informed decisions about your health.

Address Health Concerns Promptly: If you experience any unusual symptoms or health concerns, seek medical advice promptly. Early detection and intervention can prevent or manage health conditions effectively. Remember, improving physical health is a journey that requires consistency, patience, and commitment. It's essential to consult with healthcare professionals.

Mind-Body Connection: The connection between the body and mind is intricate and interdependent. The state of our physical health can significantly impact our mental well-being, and vice versa. Here are detailed explanations of the body-mind connection:

Physical Health and Mental Well-being
Neurochemicals: The body produces neurochemicals such as endorphins, dopamine, and serotonin during physical activity, which can elevate mood, reduce stress, and improve overall mental well-being.

Hormonal Balance: Regular exercise, a healthy diet, and adequate sleep help regulate hormone levels, including cortisol (the stress hormone) and melatonin (the sleep hormone), which impact our mood, stress response, and cognitive function.

Brain Health: Good physical health supports brain health by promoting efficient blood flow and oxygenation, neuroplasticity, and the production of new brain cells.

Stress Reduction: Physical activity, particularly aerobic exercise, can help reduce stress levels by promoting the release of endorphins, which act as natural stress and pain relievers.

Relaxation Techniques: Engaging in practices like yoga, meditation, or deep breathing exercises can activate the body's relaxation response, reducing the physiological and psychological effects of stress.

Cognitive Function and Mental Clarity: Regular exercise and a healthy diet improve blood circulation and oxygen delivery to the brain, enhancing cognitive function, memory, focus, and mental clarity. Adequate sleep is crucial for optimal brain function, consolidating memories, and enhancing cognitive abilities such as problem-solving, decision-making, and creativity.

Emotional Regulation: Physical activity and regular exercise contribute to emotional regulation by stimulating the release of endorphins and neurotransmitters that help regulate mood and emotions. Mindfulness practices can enhance self-awareness, allowing us to recognize and regulate our emotions more effectively.

Self-Confidence and Body Image: Taking care of our physical health can boost self-confidence and improve body image, leading to positive mental well-being. Engaging in regular physical activity and maintaining a balanced diet can help achieve and maintain a healthy weight, improve body composition, and enhance overall body satisfaction.

Holistic Approach: The body-mind connection emphasizes the importance of adopting a holistic approach to health, considering the physical, mental, and emotional aspects of well-being. Taking care of the body through proper nutrition, exercise, sleep, and self-care practices positively impacts mental health and promotes overall well-being.

Seeking Support: If you're experiencing mental health challenges, seeking professional help is essential. Mental health professionals, such as therapists or counselors, can provide guidance and interventions that address both the psychological and physical aspects of well-being.

Understanding and nurturing the body-mind connection is key to achieving holistic health and well-being. By prioritizing physical health, engaging in regular exercise, maintaining a balanced diet, managing stress, and seeking support when needed, you can foster a positive relationship between your body and mind, leading to improved overall well-being.

THE KINGDOM OF MENTAL HEALTH THERAPY

Mental health therapy is a powerful tool that offers individuals the opportunity to heal, grow, and navigate life's challenges with resilience. In a world where stress, anxiety, and emotional distress are prevalent, therapy provides a safe and supportive space for individuals to explore their thoughts, emotions, and behaviors. This article aims to shed light on the transformative potential of mental health therapy, the different approaches available, and the numerous benefits it offers.

Understanding Mental Health Therapy
a. Therapeutic Approaches: Mental health therapy encompasses various approaches tailored to meet individual needs. Some popular forms include cognitive-behavioral therapy (CBT), psychodynamic therapy, person-centered therapy, and mindfulness-based therapy. Each approach focuses on different aspects of mental health and employs unique techniques to foster healing and personal growth.

b. Professional Guidance: Mental health therapists, such as psychologists, psychiatrists, counselors, and social workers, are trained professionals who provide guidance and support throughout the therapeutic process. They create a safe and non-judgmental environment for clients to express themselves and work collaboratively towards improved mental well-being.

Benefits of Mental Health Therapy
a. Emotional Resilience: Therapy equips individuals with coping skills and emotional resilience, enabling them to navigate life's challenges more effectively. It provides tools to manage stress, regulate emotions, and develop healthier ways of relating to oneself and others.

b. Enhanced Self-Awareness: Therapy fosters self-exploration and introspection, allowing individuals to gain a deeper understanding of their thoughts, emotions, and behaviors. This self-awareness facilitates personal growth, empowers decision-making, and improves overall self-esteem and confidence.

c. Healing Trauma and Grief: Therapy provides a safe space to process and heal from traumatic experiences, grief, and loss. Therapists offer support, validation, and effective techniques to help individuals work through their pain, build resilience, and find new meaning in life.
d. Relationship Improvement: Therapy can enhance interpersonal relationships by addressing communication issues, fostering empathy, and improving conflict resolution skills. It can help individuals develop healthier boundaries, create deeper connections, and cultivate more satisfying relationships.

e. Managing Mental Health Conditions: Mental health therapy is instrumental in managing and treating various mental health conditions, including anxiety disorders, depression, post-traumatic stress disorder (PTSD), and eating disorders. Therapists provide evidence-based interventions and collaborate with individuals to develop personalized treatment plans.

f. Promoting Self-Care and Well-being: Therapy encourages individuals to prioritize self-care, promoting overall well-being. Therapists guide clients in developing healthy lifestyle habits, stress management techniques, and strategies for maintaining a balanced and fulfilling life.

Seeking Mental Health Therapy:
a. Recognizing the Need: It is essential to recognize when professional help is needed. If you are experiencing persistent emotional distress, difficulty coping with daily life, or a decline in your overall well-being, seeking therapy can be a proactive step towards healing and growth.

b. Finding the Right Therapist: Finding a compatible therapist is crucial for a successful therapeutic journey. Consider factors such as their expertise, therapeutic approach, and personality. Seek recommendations, utilize online directories, or consult with mental health professionals to find a therapist who suits your needs.

c. Overcoming Stigma: Overcoming societal stigma surrounding mental health is essential. Seeking therapy is a courageous act of self-care, and it is vital to prioritize your well-being above any perceived judgment or prejudice.

d. Commitment to the Process: Therapy requires commitment and active participation. It is a collaborative process that involves honesty, openness, and willingness to engage in self-reflection. Consistency and regular attendance to therapy sessions contribute to the effectiveness of the therapeutic process and your personal growth.

THE KINGDOM OF SOBRIETY

AVOID DRUGS LIKE THE PLAGUE: Drug addiction and substance abuse can have a profound impact on individuals, their families, and society as a whole. Here are some of the difficulties commonly associated with drug addiction and substance abuse:

Health consequences: Substance abuse can lead to a range of physical and mental health problems. Long-term drug use can damage vital organs, such as the heart, liver, and lungs. It can also increase the risk of infectious diseases like HIV/AIDS and hepatitis through needle sharing or risky behaviors. Mental health disorders, such as anxiety, depression, and psychosis, are also common among individuals struggling with substance abuse.

Impaired cognitive function: Drug addiction can adversely affect cognitive abilities, including memory, attention, decision-making, and impulse control. These cognitive impairments can make it difficult for individuals to perform well in school or at work, maintain healthy relationships, and make sound judgments.

Financial strain: Substance abuse often leads to financial difficulties. The costs associated with purchasing drugs or alcohol can drain financial resources, leading to financial instability, debt, and even poverty. Individuals may struggle to meet their basic needs, such as housing, food, and healthcare, which can further exacerbate the challenges they face.

Relationship problems: Drug addiction can strain relationships with family, friends, and romantic partners. Substance abuse can lead to broken trust, increased conflict, and emotional distance. The need to obtain and use drugs can take precedence over maintaining healthy relationships, leading to social isolation and a lack of support.

Legal issues: Substance abuse often involves engaging in illegal activities to obtain drugs or due to impaired judgment while under the influence. This can result in legal problems, such as arrests, convictions, and incarceration. Criminal records can have long-term consequences, including difficulty finding employment, securing housing, or accessing educational opportunities.

Risky behaviors and accidents: Substance abuse impairs judgment and coordination, increasing the likelihood of engaging in risky behaviors. Individuals under the influence may drive under the influence of drugs or alcohol, increasing the risk of accidents and injury to themselves and others. Additionally, drug use can impair decision-making and increase the likelihood of engaging in unsafe sexual practices, leading to an increased risk of sexually transmitted infections.

Psychological and emotional challenges: Substance abuse often co-occurs with mental health disorders, creating a complex and challenging situation. Individuals may use drugs or alcohol as a means to cope with underlying emotional or psychological issues, but the substances can exacerbate or even cause mental health problems. This cycle can make It difficult for individuals to break free from addiction and address their mental health needs effectively.

Overdose and mortality: Drug addiction carries a significant risk of overdose and death. Overdose occurs when an individual consumes a toxic amount of a substance, leading to life-threatening effects. The potency and composition of illicit drugs like fentanyl can be unpredictable, increasing the risk of overdose. Additionally, the lifestyle and behaviors associated with substance abuse can increase the likelihood of accidents and fatalities. Overcoming drug addiction and substance abuse requires comprehensive treatment approaches that address both the physical and psychological aspects of addiction. Professional interventions, support systems, and rehabilitation programs can help individuals regain control of their lives, improve their health, and rebuild relationships. In this world as we currently live, nothing has probably destroyed more Kings & Queens than drugs. Thus why, at Onassis Krown, a portion of all of our proceeds goes to help victims of substance abuse and domestic violence. Please get help for yourself or a loved one if you are suffering or know someone who is suffering from this type of addiction.

THE 5ᵀᴴ JEWEL: FAMILY

The Value of Family: Family plays a crucial role in our lives, providing a sense of belonging, support, and love. The importance of family can be seen in various aspects of our well-being and personal development. Here are detailed explanations of the importance of family in building a happy kingdom:

Emotional Support: Family members provide emotional support during challenging times, offering a safe space to express feelings, seek advice, and receive comfort. A supportive family environment helps individuals develop resilience and cope with life's ups and downs more effectively.

Unconditional Love and Acceptance: Family members offer unconditional love and acceptance, providing a sense of security and belonging. This love helps individuals develop a positive self-image and confidence in their abilities.

Identity Formation: Family plays a vital role in shaping an individual's identity. Through shared values, traditions, and cultural practices, families help individuals develop a sense of self and a connection to their heritage. Family stories, rituals, and experiences contribute to a person's understanding of their roots and provide a sense of continuity and belonging.

Supportive Relationships: Close family relationships foster healthy interpersonal skills, empathy, and communication abilities. These skills are valuable in forming and maintaining relationships beyond the family unit. Positive family relationships serve as a model for healthy relationships, helping individuals establish meaningful connections and navigate social dynamics throughout their lives.

Values and Morals: Family serves as the primary source for transmitting values, ethics, and moral principles. Parents and older family members impart important life lessons, helping individuals develop a strong moral compass and guiding their behavior and decision-making.

Education and Learning: Family involvement in education greatly influences a child's academic success and overall development. Engaged families support learning, encourage curiosity, and provide a conducive environment for intellectual growth. Family members can act as mentors, sharing knowledge and life experiences, and encouraging educational pursuits.

Health and Well-being: Supportive family environments positively impact physical and mental health. Families can promote healthy habits, such as regular exercise, balanced nutrition, and emotional well-being. Family members can provide practical support during illness or challenging times, aiding in the recovery process and reducing stress.

Lifelong Connections: Family connections often last a lifetime, providing a source of stability, companionship, and shared memories. Family gatherings, celebrations, and traditions strengthen bonds and foster a sense of belonging and unity.

Intergenerational Support: Family networks often extend across generations, providing support and care for children, parents, and grandparents. Grandparents, in particular, can offer unique wisdom, guidance, and a sense of continuity.

Legacy and Heritage: Family carries on traditions, stories, and cultural heritage, ensuring that important aspects of our history are preserved and passed down to future generations. Through family connections, individuals develop a sense of belonging to a larger legacy, contributing to their sense of identity and purpose.

It is important to note that family structures can vary greatly, and the definition of family extends beyond biological relationships to include chosen families, close friends, and supportive communities. Regardless of the specific makeup, the presence of a caring and supportive network is vital for personal growth, happiness, and overall well-being.

THE KINGDOM OF FRIENDSHIP

The Value of Friends: Friends play a significant role in our lives, providing companionship, support, and a sense of belonging. The importance of friends can be seen in various aspects of our well-being and personal growth. Here are detailed explanations of the importance of friends:

Emotional Support: Friends offer emotional support during both joyful and challenging times. They provide a listening ear, empathy, and understanding, which can help us navigate through life's ups and downs. Sharing our thoughts, feelings, and experiences with friends fosters a sense of connection, validation, and comfort.

Social Connection and Belonging: Friends contribute to our social connectedness and a sense of belonging. They provide opportunities for social interaction, engagement, and shared activities, reducing feelings of loneliness and isolation. Friendships help us build a network of like-minded individuals who share common interests, values, and goals, allowing us to feel understood and accepted.

Mental and Emotional Well-being: Positive friendships have a positive impact on our mental and emotional well-being. Friends can boost our mood, provide a sense of happiness, and enhance overall life satisfaction. Engaging in enjoyable activities with friends promotes laughter, fun, and stress relief, contributing to improved mental health.

Supportive Relationships: Friends play a significant role in our support system outside of the family. They provide a different perspective, advice, and insights on various life situations, broadening our understanding and helping us make informed decisions. Healthy friendships encourage personal growth, self-reflection, and self-improvement by providing constructive feedback, challenging us to expand our horizons, and supporting our goals and aspirations.

Shared Experiences and Memories: Friends are companions on our journey through life, sharing experiences, adventures, and memories. Together, we create lasting bonds and stories that become cherished parts of our personal narratives. Friendships provide opportunities for new and diverse experiences, introducing us to different cultures, perspectives, and interests.

Learning and Personal Development: Friends can be a source of knowledge, skills, and inspiration. They can introduce us to new ideas, hobbies, and interests, broadening our horizons and supporting our personal growth. Through friendships, we learn essential social skills such as communication, empathy, compromise, and conflict resolution, which are valuable in all areas of life.

Network and Professional Opportunities: Friends often form part of our professional network, opening doors to new career opportunities, collaborations, and mentorship. They can provide recommendations, connections, and support during job searches, career transitions, and professional development.

Celebrations and Support during Milestones: Friends are there to celebrate our achievements and milestones, offering encouragement and validation. Their presence and support enhance our joy and make special moments more meaningful.

Health and Well-being: Engaging in social activities and spending time with friends has positive effects on our physical health. It can promote an active lifestyle, encourage healthy behaviors, and provide a sense of accountability in maintaining overall well-being.

Lifelong Relationships: Friendships often endure through different stages of life, providing long-term companionship and support. Lifelong friends offer continuity and stability in a world of constant change. Cultivating and maintaining meaningful friendships requires effort, mutual respect, and genuine care. By nurturing these connections, we enhance our well-being, expand our horizons, and create a supportive network of individuals who enrich our lives in immeasurable ways.

THE KINGDOM OF DATING FOR WOMEN

Dating can be an exciting yet complex journey, especially for young girls and women who are navigating their way through the ever-evolving world of relationships. It is essential for young women to approach dating with self-assurance, self-respect, and a focus on personal growth. By fostering healthy communication, building self-esteem, setting boundaries, and prioritizing emotional well-being, young girls and women can develop effective dating strategies that empower them to make informed decisions and form fulfilling connections. This aims to provide detailed insights into dating strategies tailored specifically for young girls and women, emphasizing the importance of self-care, self-discovery, and respectful relationships.

Cultivate Self-Esteem and Confidence: Building a strong foundation of self-esteem and confidence is crucial when it comes to dating. Young girls and women should prioritize self-care, engage in activities they enjoy, and surround themselves with positive influences. By embracing their individuality and recognizing their self-worth, they become more likely to attract partners who appreciate and respect them for who they are.

Communication is Key: Effective communication lies at the heart of healthy relationships. Young girls and women should strive for open and honest communication with their partners. Expressing feelings, needs, and expectations openly helps foster understanding, trust, and emotional connection.

Clear communication allows for mutual growth and ensures that both individuals are on the same page.

Set Boundaries and Respect Them: Setting and respecting personal boundaries is essential for maintaining healthy relationships. Young girls and women should establish their boundaries early on and communicate them to their partners. Boundaries define what is acceptable and unacceptable in a relationship, protecting emotional well-being and fostering mutual respect. It is crucial to assertively enforce boundaries and recognize any red flags that may indicate a lack of respect or disregard for those boundaries.

Take Time for Self-Discovery: Dating should not be solely about finding a partner but also about self-discovery and personal growth. Young girls and women should take the time to explore their own interests, values, and goals. Engaging in self-reflection and pursuing individual passions allows them to develop a strong sense of self and create a fulfilling life independently. This self-discovery process helps in identifying compatible partners who share similar values and interests.

Seek Supportive Relationships: Surrounding oneself with a strong support system is vital during the dating process. Young girls and women should seek friends, family members, or mentors who provide guidance, encouragement, and emotional support. A supportive network helps build resilience, provides valuable insights, and offers a safe space to discuss concerns or doubts.

Prioritize Emotional Well-being: Prioritizing emotional well-being is crucial in dating. Young girls and women should take care of their mental and emotional health by engaging in self-care practices, seeking professional help when needed, and practicing self-compassion. It is important to recognize and address any signs of emotional manipulation, control, or abuse in relationships. Putting one's well-being first ensures the development of healthy and fulfilling connections.

THE KINGDOM OF DATING FOR MEN

Dating can be an exciting and sometimes challenging journey for young boys and men as they navigate the intricacies of relationships. It is crucial for young men to approach dating with self-assurance, respect for others, and a commitment to personal growth. By fostering healthy communication, building self-confidence, understanding consent and boundaries, and nurturing emotional well-being, young boys and men can develop effective dating strategies that empower them to build meaningful connections and foster respectful relationships. This aims to provide detailed insights into dating strategies tailored specifically for young boys and men, emphasizing the importance of empathy, self-reflection, and positive masculinity.

Cultivate Self-Confidence: Building self-confidence is an essential foundation for successful dating. Young boys and men should focus on personal growth, engage in activities that bring them joy and fulfillment, and develop a positive self-image. Confidence attracts others and creates a sense of ease and comfort in social interactions. Embracing one's individuality and recognizing personal strengths and qualities will contribute to a healthier dating experience.

Embrace Empathy and Active Listening: Empathy is a crucial skill for building and maintaining healthy relationships. Young boys and men should prioritize active listening, seeking to understand their partner's perspectives, feelings, and needs. By practicing empathy, they demonstrate respect and foster deeper connections. Being attentive to verbal and non-verbal cues enables better communication and helps build trust.

Understand Consent and Respect Boundaries: Understanding and respecting boundaries is fundamental in dating. Young boys and men should familiarize themselves with the concept of consent and ensure that all interactions are consensual. It is important to recognize that consent can be withdrawn at any time and should always be enthusiastic and ongoing. Respecting personal boundaries shows maturity and establishes a foundation of trust and respect within relationships.

Challenge Stereotypes and Embrace Positive Masculinity: Young boys and men should challenge traditional gender stereotypes and embrace positive masculinity. Positive masculinity involves rejecting harmful attitudes and behaviors such as aggression, dominance, and emotional suppression. Instead, they should promote qualities like emotional intelligence, vulnerability, respect, and equality in relationships. By embracing positive masculinity, young men foster healthier dynamics, create safer spaces, and nurture more fulfilling connections.

Communicate Openly and Honestly: Effective communication is essential for healthy relationships. Young boys and men should practice open and honest communication with their partners. Expressing feelings, desires, and concerns openly and respectfully helps build trust and understanding. Clear communication also allows for resolving conflicts and addressing any issues that may arise, fostering a stronger and more meaningful connection.

Prioritize Emotional Well-being: Prioritizing emotional well-being is crucial for young boys and men in the dating process. They should engage in self-care activities, seek support from friends or mentors, and recognize the importance of managing emotions in a healthy way. Taking care of one's mental and emotional health ensures a solid foundation for building and maintaining relationships based on mutual respect and understanding.

Dating can be a transformative and empowering experience for young boys and men when approached with self-confidence, empathy, and a commitment to personal growth. By cultivating self-confidence, embracing empathy and active listening, understanding consent and boundaries, challenging stereotypes, promoting positive masculinity, practicing open communication, and prioritizing emotional well-being, young boys and men can develop effective dating strategies that foster healthy and respectful relationships. Remember, true strength lies in embracing vulnerability, empathy, and open communication. Approach dating as an opportunity for personal growth, learning, and building connections based on equality and respect.

THE KINGDOM OF SEX

Engaging in sexual activity is a natural and personal choice, but it is essential to be aware of the potential risks involved, particularly when it comes to unprotected sex. Unprotected sex refers to sexual activity without the use of barrier methods such as condoms or other forms of contraception. While it is crucial to promote comprehensive sex education and open conversations about sexual health, this article aims to provide a detailed exploration of the risks associated with unprotected sex. By understanding the potential consequences, individuals can make informed decisions, prioritize their sexual health, and take necessary precautions to protect themselves and their partners.

Unwanted Pregnancy: One of the significant risks of unprotected sex is the potential for unintended pregnancy. Without the use of contraception, the chances of conception increase significantly. Unplanned pregnancies can have far-reaching emotional, financial, and social implications for individuals and couples. It is essential for sexually active individuals to discuss and explore contraceptive options to prevent unwanted pregnancies and consider the use of condoms, hormonal methods, or other forms of birth control.

Sexually Transmitted Infections (STIs): Engaging in unprotected sex puts individuals at a higher risk of contracting sexually transmitted infections (STIs). STIs such as chlamydia, gonorrhea, syphilis, herpes, human papillomavirus (HPV), and human immunodeficiency virus (HIV) can be transmitted through sexual contact. These infections can have serious health consequences, ranging from discomfort and pain to long-term health complications. The consistent and correct use of condoms, along with regular STI testing, can significantly reduce the risk of transmission.

HIV/AIDS: Human immunodeficiency virus (HIV) is a particularly concerning STI due to its potential progression to acquired immunodeficiency syndrome (AIDS). Unprotected sexual intercourse, particularly with an infected partner, significantly increases the risk of HIV transmission. HIV weakens the immune system, making individuals more susceptible to other infections and illnesses. It is crucial to use condoms consistently and undergo regular HIV testing, especially if engaging in high-risk behaviors or if unsure of a partner's HIV status.

Emotional Consequences: Unprotected sex can also have emotional consequences. Engaging in intimate activities without protection can lead to feelings of regret, guilt, anxiety, or fear about potential pregnancy or contracting STIs. Emotional well-being is just as important as physical health, and it is essential to consider these aspects when making decisions about sexual activity. Open and honest communication with sexual partners, as well as seeking support from healthcare professionals or counselors, can help address emotional concerns associated with unprotected sex.

Fertility and Reproductive Health: Unprotected sex can have implications for long-term fertility and reproductive health. Some STIs, such as chlamydia and gonorrhea, can cause pelvic inflammatory disease (PID) in females if left untreated. PID can lead to scarring of the reproductive organs, increasing the risk of infertility or ectopic pregnancies. It is vital for individuals to prioritize regular STI testing, seek treatment if necessary, and utilize barrier methods or other contraception to protect their reproductive health.

Relationship Implications: Unprotected sex can have significant implications for relationships. Trust and communication play a crucial role in sexual relationships, especially when it comes to decisions about contraception and protection. Engaging in unprotected sex without prior discussion or agreement with a partner can lead to conflicts, misunderstandings, or breaches of trust. It is important for individuals to have open and honest conversations about sexual health, boundaries, and contraceptive methods to ensure the well-being and trust within the relationship. Understanding the risks associated with unprotected sex is vital for individuals to make informed decisions about their sexual health.

THE KINGDOM OF PRE-COHABITATING COUNSELING

Taking the leap to move in together is an exciting milestone for couples. However, cohabitation comes with its own set of challenges as two individuals merge their lives, routines, and habits. To ensure a smooth transition and establish a strong foundation, pre-cohabiting counseling plays a pivotal role. In this article, we delve into the importance of seeking professional guidance before embarking on this significant journey together.

Understanding Cohabitation: Cohabitation refers to the act of living together as a couple without being married. It can be an enriching experience, deepening the bond between partners and fostering personal growth. However, it is not without its complexities. By seeking pre-cohabiting counseling, couples can navigate potential obstacles, address concerns, and establish healthy communication patterns, fostering a successful cohabitation experience.

Enhancing Communication: Effective communication is vital for any relationship, and cohabitation amplifies its significance. Through pre-cohabiting counseling, couples can develop communication skills that enable them to express their needs, concerns, and expectations openly. Learning constructive ways to address conflicts, negotiate compromises, and set boundaries can prevent misunderstandings and foster a harmonious living environment.

Managing Expectations: Cohabitation often entails blending lifestyles, routines, and habits. Each partner brings their unique set of expectations, which can lead to unforeseen conflicts if not addressed proactively. Pre-cohabiting counseling allows couples to have open discussions about their expectations regarding finances, household responsibilities, personal space, and long-term goals. These conversations help align expectations and avoid future conflicts.

Exploring Values and Beliefs: Cohabitation can bring underlying values and beliefs to the surface. Pre-cohabiting counseling provides a safe space for couples to explore their cultural, religious, and moral backgrounds. Understanding each other's perspectives and finding common ground builds a strong foundation and promotes mutual respect, acceptance, and tolerance.

Financial Planning: Sharing living expenses and financial responsibilities is a crucial aspect of cohabitation. Pre-cohabiting counseling equips couples with the necessary tools to have candid conversations about finances, including budgeting, bill payments, and savings goals. Addressing financial concerns early on helps establish a sense of financial security and prevents conflicts related to money matters.

Balancing Independence and Togetherness: Cohabitation requires finding a healthy balance between personal independence and shared experiences. Pre-cohabiting counseling assists couples in identifying their individual needs for personal space, hobbies, and socializing while fostering a sense of togetherness. It encourages couples to develop strategies that support individual growth within the context of a shared living arrangement.

Preparing for Future Commitments: Cohabitation often serves as a precursor to marriage or long-term commitment. Pre-cohabiting counseling can act as a steppingstone, preparing couples for the next stage of their relationship. By addressing potential challenges early on, couples can develop skills and strategies that will serve them well in the future, fostering a strong and lasting bond.

Pre-cohabiting counseling offers couples an invaluable opportunity to build a solid foundation before embarking on the journey of living together. By addressing communication, expectations, values, finances, and personal growth, couples can lay the groundwork for a harmonious and fulfilling cohabitation experience. Seeking professional guidance demonstrates a commitment to nurturing a healthy relationship, enhancing the likelihood of long-term success and happiness. Remember, investing time and effort in pre-cohabiting counseling is an investment in the future of your relationship.

THE KINGDOM OF CHILDREN BEARING

While having children in the context of marriage may be more ideal, the reality is that many people are having children before marriage so we wanted to at least broach the conversation of people having children without being married to the co-parent. The decision to have children is a deeply personal one, and it is essential to consider the long-term implications and responsibilities that come with parenting. When children are born to multiple partners, it can present unique challenges and potential disadvantages for both parents and children involved. This article aims to provide a detailed exploration of the disadvantages associated with having children with multiple partners. By understanding these potential challenges, individuals can make informed choices and navigate the complexities of co-parenting, emphasizing the well-being and stability of the children involved.

Emotional and Psychological Impact on Children: Having children with multiple partners can impact the emotional and psychological well-being of the children involved. Growing up in a complex family structure may lead to confusion, feelings of instability, and a lack of a cohesive family identity. Children may struggle with questions about their identity, sense of belonging, and their place within multiple households. This can potentially affect their self-esteem, emotional development, and overall well-being.

Challenges in Co-Parenting: Coordinating parenting responsibilities and maintaining healthy communication among multiple partners can be challenging. Differences in parenting styles, values, and priorities may create conflicts and disagreements, making it difficult to establish consistent rules and routines for the children. Inconsistent or conflicting parenting approaches can cause confusion for children and impact their sense of stability and security.

Financial Strain: Raising children can be costly, and having children with multiple partners can amplify financial strain. Each parent may have separate financial obligations and responsibilities, potentially leading to uneven distribution of financial resources.

This can impact the quality of life for the children and create disparities in access to educational opportunities, healthcare, and other essential resources.

Time Management and Balancing Responsibilities: Juggling multiple parenting responsibilities and coordinating schedules can be demanding for both parents and children. It may become challenging to allocate quality time, attention, and support to each child, particularly when the children reside in different households. This can potentially impact the depth and quality of the parent-child relationships, as well as the overall well-being and development of the children.

Potential Conflict and Instability: Having children with multiple partners can introduce complex dynamics and potential conflicts within extended families. Interactions between parents, step-parents, and siblings from different relationships can be challenging to navigate, leading to tension and potential instability. Children may witness or be exposed to disagreements, conflicts, or unresolved issues, which can have a negative impact on their emotional well-being and sense of security.

Impact on Future Relationships: The presence of children from multiple partners can influence future relationships for both parents. Potential partners may have concerns about the complexities of the family structure, the level of involvement and commitment required, and the potential for conflicts or competition among parents. It is essential to consider the impact of this dynamic on future romantic relationships and the potential challenges it may pose for creating a stable and harmonious family unit.

While the decision to have children is a deeply personal one, it is important to recognize and understand the potential disadvantages associated with having children with multiple partners. Emotional and psychological impacts on children, challenges in co-parenting, financial strain, time management difficulties, potential conflict and instability, and the impact on future relationships are all factors that should be carefully considered. Open and honest communication, establishing clear boundaries, prioritizing the well-being of the children involved, and seeking support from professionals or support networks can help navigate the complexities and minimize the potential disadvantages associated with parenting children from multiple partners.

THE KINGDOM OF PRE-MARITAL COUNSELING

Entering into marriage is a significant life milestone filled with excitement and anticipation. However, it is essential to recognize that building a strong and lasting marital foundation requires intentional effort and preparation. Pre-marital counseling offers a valuable opportunity for couples to explore and address key aspects of their relationship, enhance communication skills, navigate potential challenges, and set realistic expectations. This article aims to highlight the value of pre-marital counseling and its potential to foster a healthy and thriving marriage.

Improved Communication and Conflict Resolution Skills: Effective communication is the cornerstone of a successful marriage. Pre-marital counseling equips couples with essential communication tools, helping them express their thoughts, feelings, and needs more effectively. Through counseling sessions, couples learn active listening, conflict resolution, and negotiation skills, enabling them to navigate disagreements and maintain open, respectful communication in their marriage.

Identifying Strengths and Growth Areas: Pre-marital counseling provides a safe space for couples to reflect on their individual strengths and areas for growth. Professional counselors guide couples through assessments, discussions, and activities to help them gain insight into their personality traits, values, and expectations. Understanding each other's strengths and growth areas allows couples to build on their strengths and address potential challenges before they arise.

Establishing Realistic Expectations: Unrealistic expectations can lead to disappointment and frustration in a marriage. Pre-marital counseling assists couples in exploring and aligning their expectations regarding various aspects of married life, such as roles and responsibilities, finances, parenting, and intimacy. By addressing these expectations early on, couples can develop a shared understanding and negotiate compromises, fostering a healthier and more harmonious partnership.

Addressing Past Relationship Patterns: Many individuals bring patterns from past relationships into their marriage, consciously or unconsciously. Pre-marital counseling provides a platform for couples to explore and address any unresolved issues, traumas, or negative relationship patterns from their past. By acknowledging and working through these challenges, couples can break unhealthy cycles and create a stronger foundation for their future together.

Strengthening Emotional Intimacy: Building emotional intimacy is vital for a fulfilling and connected marriage. Pre-marital counseling helps couples enhance their emotional bond by fostering vulnerability, empathy, and trust. Couples learn strategies to deepen their emotional connection, express affection, and understand each other's emotional needs. This strengthened emotional intimacy lays the groundwork for a supportive and loving marital relationship.

Preparation for Potential Challenges: No marriage is without challenges, but pre-marital counseling equips couples with the tools and knowledge to navigate them successfully. Couples explore topics such as managing conflict, maintaining a healthy work-life balance, and handling stressors that commonly arise in marriages. By being prepared and having a proactive approach, couples are better equipped to face challenges together, minimizing their impact on the relationship.

Commitment to Long-Term Relationship Success: Engaging in pre-marital counseling demonstrates a shared commitment to the long-term success of the relationship. By investing time and effort before marriage, couples prioritize their relationship and set a foundation for ongoing growth and development. Pre-marital counseling encourages couples to continually nurture their connection and seek support when needed, fostering a resilient and lasting marriage.

Pre-marital counseling offers invaluable benefits to couples preparing for marriage. By providing a supportive and structured environment, pre-marital counseling helps couples enhance their communication skills, identify strengths and growth areas, establish realistic expectations, address past relationship patterns, strengthen emotional intimacy, prepare for potential challenges, and demonstrate commitment to long-term relationship success. Investing in pre-marital counseling not only sets couples up for a more fulfilling and resilient marriage but also promotes a deeper understanding of each other and lays the groundwork for a lifelong journey of love and partnership.

THE KINGDOM OF MARRIAGE

Marriage: Marriage is a significant and complex institution that comes with various benefits and challenges. While the experience of marriage can differ for each couple, here are detailed explanations of the benefits and challenges commonly associated with marriage:

Benefits of Marriage
Emotional Support and Companionship: Marriage provides a deep emotional bond and companionship, offering a partner with whom to share joys, sorrows, and life's experiences. Having a spouse who understands and supports you can enhance emotional well-being and provide a sense of belonging and security.

Partnership and Shared Responsibilities: Marriage involves creating a partnership where both individuals share responsibilities, making it easier to manage day-to-day tasks, financial obligations, and household chores. Sharing responsibilities allows for a more efficient division of labor, providing mutual support and reducing individual burdens.

Intimacy and Sexual Fulfillment: Marriage typically involves a committed and intimate relationship, allowing for the expression of physical affection, emotional intimacy, and sexual fulfillment. The emotional connection and trust developed in a marital relationship can contribute to a more satisfying and fulfilling sexual life.

Financial Stability and Security: Marriage often provides financial stability through shared resources, combined incomes, and joint financial planning. Couples can pool their resources, making it easier to manage expenses, plan for the future, and achieve financial goals.

Emotional and Health Benefits: Research suggests that married individuals generally experience better mental and physical health outcomes compared to unmarried individuals. The emotional support, companionship, and stability found in a marital relationship can contribute to lower stress levels, improved overall health, and a longer life expectancy.

Parenting and Family Life: Marriage often leads to starting a family, providing the opportunity to raise children together and create a supportive and nurturing environment for them. Sharing the responsibilities of parenting allows for shared decision-making, mutual support, and the ability to provide a stable and loving family unit for children.

Challenges of Marriage
Communication and Conflict Resolution: Effective communication and conflict resolution are essential in any marriage. Differences in communication styles, disagreements, and conflicts can pose challenges that require open and honest dialogue to resolve. Learning effective communication skills and developing conflict resolution strategies are crucial for maintaining a healthy and harmonious marital relationship.

Adjusting to Differences and Individual Growth: Marriage requires individuals to navigate and embrace differences in personalities, backgrounds, beliefs, and expectations. As individuals grow and change over time, it is essential to adapt to these changes, support each other's personal growth, and find a balance between individuality and togetherness.

Balancing Individual and Shared Needs: Balancing individual needs and desires with the needs of the partnership can be a challenge in marriage. Negotiating compromises and finding ways to meet both individual and shared goals is crucial for maintaining a healthy and fulfilling marriage.

Managing Stress and Life Transitions: Life transitions such as career changes, relocation, starting a family, or caring for aging parents can create stress and strain within a marriage. Managing these transitions effectively requires communication, adaptability, and support from both partners.

Maintaining Intimacy and Connection: Over time, the excitement and novelty in a marriage may evolve, and couples may need to put effort into maintaining emotional and physical intimacy. Sustaining connection and intimacy may require open communication, shared activities, and finding new ways to keep the spark alive.

Commitment and Long-term Investment: Marriage requires a long-term commitment and investment of time, effort, and energy from both partners. Staying committed to the relationship, nurturing the emotional connection, and working through challenges together are essential.

THE KINGDOM OF EMPLOYMENT

In today's fast-paced world, securing stable employment has become a crucial aspect of maintaining household stability. Working a job provides numerous benefits beyond just financial security. It contributes to personal growth, a sense of purpose, and overall family well-being. This article aims to explore the advantages of working a job for household stability, emphasizing the positive impact on financial security, personal development, and the overall stability of the family unit.

Financial Security and Stability: One of the most significant benefits of working a job is the financial security it provides. A steady income helps cover daily expenses, mortgage or rent payments, utility bills, and other essential needs. It enables individuals and families to plan for the future, save for emergencies, and invest in long-term goals, such as education, retirement, or homeownership. Financial stability offers peace of mind, reducing stress and ensuring a solid foundation for the household.

Increased Independence and Self-Sufficiency: Working a job fosters independence and self-sufficiency within individuals and households. It allows individuals to rely on their own abilities to support themselves and contribute to the family's financial well-being. Economic independence empowers individuals to make decisions and choices that align with their values and aspirations, enhancing their overall sense of self-worth and fulfillment.

Expanded Opportunities for Professional Growth: A job provides an avenue for personal and professional development. By engaging in meaningful work, individuals can enhance their skills, acquire new knowledge, and gain valuable experience. Professional growth often leads to increased job satisfaction, higher earning potential, and potential career advancement opportunities. Advancing one's career can positively impact the financial stability of the household, opening doors for additional benefits and opportunities.

Role Modeling for Children: Working a job sets a positive example for children by demonstrating the importance of hard work, dedication, and responsibility. Children observe the value of financial independence and witness the rewards that come with working diligently. Such role modeling encourages a strong work ethic and instills essential life skills, providing a solid foundation for their future success.

Access to Employee Benefits and Social Support: Many jobs offer employee benefits that contribute to household stability. These benefits may include health insurance, retirement plans, paid time off, and educational assistance. Access to such benefits helps safeguard against unexpected medical expenses, provides retirement security, and supports personal and professional development. Furthermore, jobs often provide access to social support networks, fostering a sense of belonging and connection within the community.

Enhanced Mental and Emotional Well-being: Working a job can have positive effects on mental and emotional well-being. It provides a sense of purpose, boosts self-esteem, and promotes personal fulfillment. Engaging in meaningful work and having a structured routine can contribute to overall life satisfaction and mental well-being. Additionally, the social interactions and sense of camaraderie in the workplace can provide a support system and alleviate feelings of isolation or loneliness.

Strengthened Relationships and Household Dynamics: Working a job can enhance family relationships and household dynamics. Shared financial responsibilities promote open communication, cooperation, and joint decision-making. It fosters a sense of teamwork, ensuring all family members contribute to the household's stability and well-being. The shared sense of accomplishment and financial security can strengthen bonds and promote a harmonious living environment.

Working a job plays a crucial role in maintaining household stability. Beyond financial security, it offers numerous benefits, including increased independence, personal growth, role modeling for children, access to employee benefits and social support, enhanced mental and emotional well-being, and strengthened relationships. Engaging in meaningful work empowers individuals, promotes financial well-being, and contributes to the overall stability and prosperity of the household. By recognizing the value of employment, individuals can actively pursue opportunities that align with who they are along with their life's purpose in establishing, supporting their family and living their best lives.

THE KINGDOM OF
ENTREPRENEURSHIP & BUSINESS OWNERSHIP

Entrepreneurship and owning a business offer a unique path to financial independence, personal fulfillment, and household stability. While entrepreneurship comes with its challenges and risks, it also brings forth numerous benefits that can significantly impact a household's dynamics. This article aims to explore the multifaceted impact of entrepreneurship and owning a business on a household, highlighting the advantages of financial growth, flexibility, personal development, and the potential for long-term prosperity.

Financial Growth and Stability: Entrepreneurship provides an opportunity for substantial financial growth. Owning a successful business allows individuals to generate income beyond traditional employment, potentially increasing their earning potential and overall wealth. It opens avenues for exploring new markets, expanding services, and securing diverse revenue streams. Successful entrepreneurship can result in long-term financial stability for the household, creating opportunities for investment, savings, and future financial security.

Flexibility and Work-Life Balance: Entrepreneurship offers the advantage of flexibility and the ability to create a work-life balance that suits individual preferences and family needs. As a business owner, one can set their own schedule, allowing for increased control over time management. This flexibility enables entrepreneurs to spend more quality time with family, attend important events, and maintain a healthier work-life integration. It promotes a sense of autonomy and freedom to design a lifestyle that aligns with personal and familial goals.

Personal Development and Skill Enhancement: Owning a business provides numerous opportunities for personal growth and skill enhancement. Entrepreneurship requires individuals to develop a diverse skill set, encompassing leadership, problem-solving, decision-making, and adaptability. The challenges and responsibilities that come with running a business encourage continuous learning and personal development. Entrepreneurs often acquire valuable expertise, experience, and networking opportunities that can extend beyond their business ventures, positively influencing their personal and professional lives.

Job Creation and Community Impact: Entrepreneurship has a profound impact beyond individual households. Owning a business often involves job creation, stimulating local economies, and contributing to community development. By employing others, entrepreneurs provide opportunities for livelihood, economic stability, and personal growth for their employees. A thriving business can contribute to the overall well-being of the community, fostering a positive cycle of prosperity and improving the quality of life for individuals and households in the area.

Creative Expression and Purpose: Entrepreneurship allows individuals to pursue their passions, interests, and creative ideas. Owning a business provides an avenue for self-expression and the ability to build a venture based on personal values and beliefs. Entrepreneurs have the freedom to innovate, create unique products or services, and make a difference in their industry. The ability to align one's work with personal passions and purpose brings a sense of fulfillment and satisfaction, positively impacting not only the individual but the household as a whole.

Resilience and Risk Management: Entrepreneurship necessitates the development of resilience and risk management skills. Business ownership inherently involves taking risks, overcoming setbacks, and navigating uncertainty. Entrepreneurs learn to adapt to changing market conditions, identify opportunities, and make strategic decisions. These skills translate into other aspects of life, allowing individuals to effectively manage challenges, embrace change, and develop a resilient mindset, ultimately benefiting the household's stability and growth.

Legacy Building and Long-Term Prosperity: Entrepreneurship provides an opportunity to create a lasting legacy. A successful business can become a valuable asset that can be passed down to future generations, securing the long-term prosperity of the household. Entrepreneurs have the ability to build a brand, establish a reputation, and leave a positive impact on their industry and community. Creating a sustainable business model fosters financial security and generational wealth, potentially leaving a lasting legacy.

THE KINGDOM OF MARRIAGE COUNSELING

The Value of Marriage Counseling: Marriage counseling, also known as couples therapy or relationship counseling, is a valuable form of professional support that aims to improve and strengthen marital relationships. It involves working with a trained therapist who helps couples navigate challenges, improve communication, and foster healthier dynamics. Here is a more detailed explanation of the value of marriage counseling:

Improved Communication and Conflict Resolution: One of the primary benefits of marriage counseling is the improvement of communication patterns between partners. Therapists provide a safe and neutral space for couples to express their thoughts, feelings, and concerns openly. Through guided discussions and techniques, couples learn effective communication skills and strategies for resolving conflicts constructively.

Enhanced Relationship Satisfaction: Marriage counseling can significantly contribute to increased relationship satisfaction. By addressing underlying issues and improving communication, couples gain a better understanding of each other's needs, desires, and expectations. Therapists help couples identify and build upon the strengths of their relationship, fostering a deeper emotional connection and overall satisfaction.

Strengthened Emotional Connection: Marriage counseling aims to strengthen the emotional bond between partners. Therapists help couples identify and address emotional barriers that may be impacting their relationship. Through exercises, interventions, and guided discussions, couples develop empathy, understanding, and emotional attunement, fostering a deeper connection.

Resolving Specific Relationship Challenges: Marriage counseling provides a structured approach to address specific challenges within the relationship. Whether dealing with infidelity, trust issues, sexual difficulties, parenting conflicts, or financial disagreements, therapists can guide couples in finding constructive solutions. The therapist's expertise and neutral perspective can help couples navigate complex issues and explore alternatives to promote healing and growth.

Developing Healthy Relationship Patterns: Marriage counseling helps couples develop healthier relationship patterns and behaviors. Therapists assist in identifying negative patterns, such as criticism, defensiveness, or avoidance, and provide tools to replace them with positive and adaptive behaviors. Couples learn to cultivate qualities like empathy, active listening, and compromise, which contribute to a healthier and more satisfying relationship.

Preemptive Maintenance and Prevention: Marriage counseling is not solely for couples in crisis but can be valuable as a preventive measure. Regular counseling sessions can help couples address minor issues before they escalate into more significant problems. Couples can proactively work on maintaining their relationship's health and prevent future challenges by learning effective communication and problem-solving skills.

Safe Space for Expression and Reflection: Marriage counseling offers a safe and supportive environment for both partners to express themselves freely. The therapist acts as a neutral mediator, ensuring that both individuals are heard and validated. This safe space allows for self-reflection, understanding, and personal growth, as well as the exploration of underlying emotions and motivations.

Professional Guidance and Expertise: Marriage counselors are trained professionals with expertise in relationship dynamics and interventions. They provide guidance, tools, and evidence-based techniques tailored to the specific needs of each couple. Therapists draw upon their knowledge and experience to help couples navigate challenges, gain new perspectives, and develop healthier relationship patterns.

It's important to note that marriage counseling is most effective when both partners are committed to the process and willing to work on the relationship. The value of marriage counseling lies in its ability to provide a supportive and structured framework for couples to address challenges, strengthen their bond, and foster a healthier and more fulfilling relationship.

THE KINGDOM OF SHOTCLOCK

SHOTCLOCK TECHNIQUE:

Here is a technique for couples who have a difficult time communicating. If you're in a relationship where you sometimes argue, talk over each other, scream or shout then this method may help you to better communicate. So, for starters, a lot of times arguments seem to arise unexpectedly out of nowhere. So, if you're in a discussion and you sense it starting to go downhill then either partner can immediately call "shot clock" as a safeword.

The moment either partner says "shot clock" then both parties will immediately pull out their cellphones. One partner sets a timer for 30 minutes and the other for 2 minutes. Both parties can grab pen & paper if helpful. Choose which partner gets to speak first. You can flip a coin if necessary. Once determined who's going first, you start both timers. The first spouse gets to speak their mind for up to two minutes. The other spouse must remain quiet the entire time. The listening partner should try to refrain from making unhelpful noises, faces or reactions and should try to earnestly listen to what the speaking partner is sharing. The listening partner should take notes if need be, in order to respond to what the first speaking partner is sharing. When the 2-minute timer goes off then the speaking partner should stop speaking mid-sentence if need be.

Now the second partner gets to speak/respond for 2 minutes. Each partner should go back and forth like this speaking for two minutes at a time until the 30-minute timer goes off. If the partners have not been able to resolve the matter in the 30 minutes allowed, then both parties agree to take a 15-minute break. During the 15-minute break, each party should go get some water, use the bathroom, take a walk, watch a little tv or whatever is helpful to decompress and bring the emotions down. Once the 15 minutes is up then the two partners can do another

30-minute session sticking to the 2-minute intervals to speak.

If the second 30-minute speaking session still isn't enough to resolve the issue, then take another 15-minute break. After the second 15-minute break, both parties can attempt a third 30-minute session. This will add up to a total of an hour and a half of communicating in total. If after 3 sessions, you still are not able to resolve the matter then both parties agree to leave it alone for 24 hours. Try to go about the remainder of your day, taking care of whatever responsibilities you need to. Try to enjoy each other's company if possible but if not then simply try to keep distance between each other. Generally, after a night's sleep and 24 hours having passed, most couples don't feel the need to revisit the matter but if you feel like it is still unresolved but still important then you can attempt another "shot clock" session of the 3 intervals of speaking and breaks for a total of 1.5 hours' worth of communicating. You can do this for as many days as needed. The goal isn't necessarily to agree on the issue at hand but to improve the communication and respect for speaking and listening. Sometimes we may just never agree on an issue, but we may come to agree to disagree. Hopefully there a sincere effort to try to understand one another and respect each other's perspectives.

THE KINGDOM OF MARRIAGE MEETINGS

MARRIAGE MEETING:

If you are married or in a significant relationship and are not currently holding marriage meetings, then I encourage you to start immediately. A marriage meeting is a proactive tool to help improve your relationship and communication. It will also help set the stage for creating the relationship you desire. The marriage meeting consists of four parts: 1. Appreciation 2. Fun Planning 3. Chores/Responsibilities and 4. Challenges. You should aim to keep the entire marriage meeting limited to roughly 30-45 minutes. The last part, Challenges, tends to be the most challenging (no pun intended) and time-consuming. If you've ever heard the expression, "how do you eat an elephant?" the answer is – one bite at a time. Likewise, the goal isn't to tackle every challenge you've ever had in your relationship in one meeting.

As they say, "Rome wasn't built in a day." Try address no more than 1 – 2 challenges in a meeting. You can save any others for another meeting. You will want to use a pen & pad to take notes and this will also help as a starting point of review for future meetings. Speaking of which, you will ideally want to conduct these meetings once a week on the same day and time. If all is well, then you can eventually scale the frequency of the meetings back to once every other week or even once a month. However, if you find yourself going through a rough patch in your relationship then you can increase the number and frequency of marriage meetings as need be. So here is how each of the four parts of the marriage meetings should go:

1. Appreciation: This is merely an opportunity to recognize and appreciate one another for your contributions to the marriage/relationship. This helps to start the meeting off on a positive note as well as allow each party to let their guard down and be more receptive when we get to the challenges part. To show appreciation, simply share 5 things you appreciate about the other. It ideally will be something they've done in the past week that may have gone unnoticed at the time. Perhaps someone made dinner or picked up dinner. Maybe someone did the laundry, washed the dishes, mowed the lawn, washed the car, filled the tank up with gas, gave the other a head rub, etc. It doesn't have to be anything earth-shattering.

We just want to get in the habit of appreciating, being grateful, not taking the other's small contributions for granted and simply get comfortable saying "thank you" for being you and all the little things you do. You will be amazed at how simple recognition makes each person feel. This attitude of gratitude will also start to show itself in other areas of your life like at work, with family & friends, etc. Those who appreciate more of what they already have in life tend to attract more good will and fortune in their lives.

2. Fun Planning: To keep the positive vibes flowing, we now want to plan some fun and/or quality time with one another. Again, it doesn't have to be anything super elaborate. You just want to plan some fun times with one another. It may include children if necessary but, if possible, you want it to be just time for one another if you can get a babysitter or at least put the kids to bed at a certain time. Your something fun for the week can be simply watching a show you both enjoy together. It can be a board game or card game. It can be to go bowling, shoot pool, go to the movie theater, or watch a movie at home. It can be a dinner date, a walk through the park, a beach visit or whatever you two may find enjoyable.

One important note about the fun time is to not discuss anything heavy about the relationship or marriage. Try to avoid past issues or bring up controversial issues. Avoid making snide remarks or comments that you know may set the other person off. Just try to be cordial, friendly and in an overall good mood. This will help us to understand how to draw boundaries and know that there is a time and place for everything and if your intention was to enjoy each other's company then don't sabotage your own fun.

3. Chores/Responsibilities: For some relationships, taking care of responsibilities can be a sore spot. There are times where one party feels they're carrying a heavier burden than the other. We should avoid comparison, competition, or a tug-of-war with one another. In my experience, each person normally feels very justified with what they're bringing to the table in terms of their contribution. Perhaps one is the primary bread winner while the other is doing most of the child rearing. Maybe one does more around the house cleaning inside while the other maintains the outside or the cars or the bills. The key is to know that you are a team.

You two are both responsible for running the "business" of your relationship. So, for this part of the marriage meeting, you don't want to tell the other person what to do. Rather you want to share the things that need to be done in the upcoming week that you feel you can take care of. Give the other spouse the opportunity to share what chores they intend to do. If you recognize that something is being overlooked or forgotten, then politely bring it up and see if someone can volunteer to take care of it. If not, then determine its importance and if it is something that needs to be urgently addressed or if it can wait.

Again, this is designed to improve communication, how we seek resolutions and share responsibilities. Depending on the circumstances, there may be times when one partner is shouldering more burden than the other but "different" doesn't always mean "more." Perhaps one person's chore isn't done as often as the other, i.e., laundry versus the lawn. While clothes may need to be washed more frequently, working outside in the hot sun cutting grass, hedges, edging, etc. isn't exactly pleasant either even if it only happens once a week. If ever in doubt, try switching roles for a time and see what it feels like to be in the other's shoes. The goal, again, is to simply discuss and be aware of the household chores that need to be taken care of on a regular basis.

4. Challenges: Hopefully, if we went through the first 3 steps without incident, they went smoothly and we're in a good frame of mind to discuss challenges.

Please try to stick to the steps of this marriage meeting especially in the beginning as the order is important to improve receptivity. Again, we're not trying to tackle every challenge you've ever had. Also be aware that some "challenges" like infidelity, trust, substance abuse, etc. are going to be bigger than others and may take professional help and a lot of time to see progress. The hope is that both parties are getting better at communicating concerns at the right time without leading to arguments and nasty exchanges. Those only help to worsen the problem.

We want to address no more than one or two challenges per meeting. If an issue was unresolved then we can pick it back up from a prior meeting. If we find ourselves having difficulty discussing a matter then you can incorporate the "shot clock" technique where each party gets two minutes to talk and go back and forth like this for up to 30 minutes. For a marriage meeting, I would not recommend doing more than 30 minutes of discussing challenges. I would try to hold off until the next marriage meeting to continue the conversation. In all, using this step-by-step process should help you two to be more proactive in crystallizing the type of relationship you both desire and charting a course on how to get there.

THE KINGDOM OF WORKING SPOUSE(S)

In today's evolving society, the dynamics of households have witnessed significant changes, particularly regarding the number of working spouses. Traditionally, a one-working spouse household was more common, with one partner focusing on domestic responsibilities while the other pursued a career. However, the rise of dual-income households, where both partners work, has become increasingly prevalent. This article aims to provide a detailed exploration of the advantages and considerations associated with both one-working spouse and two-working spouses households. By understanding the dynamics and implications of each arrangement, individuals can make informed decisions that align with their values, goals, and family dynamics.

ONE-WORKING SPOUSE HOUSEHOLD

Financial Stability and Division of Labor: In a one-working spouse household, having a single income can provide a sense of financial stability. It allows for better financial planning and potentially reduces stress related to financial uncertainties. Additionally, the division of labor is more clearly defined, with one partner primarily responsible for generating income, while the other focuses on domestic responsibilities, such as managing the household, childcare, and other caregiving duties.

Parental Involvement and Flexibility: With one partner dedicated to domestic responsibilities, there is often more opportunity for increased parental involvement and quality time with children. The non-working spouse can assume a primary caregiving role, ensuring consistency and support for the children's upbringing. This arrangement may also provide flexibility in managing household tasks and responding to family needs promptly.

Career Advancement and Personal Fulfillment: In a one-working spouse household, the working partner can focus more on their career, pursuing advancement opportunities and professional development. With a clear delineation of roles, the non-working spouse can devote time and energy to personal pursuits, hobbies, or further education. This can contribute to personal fulfillment and individual growth.

TWO-WORKING SPOUSES HOUSEHOLD
Financial Independence and Shared Responsibilities: In a two-working spouses' household, both partners contribute to the family's financial stability. This arrangement can provide a greater sense of financial independence and shared responsibility, with both partners contributing to financial planning, decision-making, and achieving common goals. It can also offer a greater financial cushion and increased flexibility in managing expenses.

Equitable Division of Domestic Duties: In a two-working spouses' household, there is a greater emphasis on sharing domestic responsibilities. Both partners participate in managing household chores, childcare, and other caregiving duties. This equitable distribution of responsibilities can foster a sense of teamwork, collaboration, and mutual support, reducing the burden on any one individual.

Professional Fulfillment and Personal Growth: Having two working spouses can provide an environment that supports the pursuit of professional fulfillment and personal growth for both individuals. Each partner can develop their career, pursue individual goals, and experience personal satisfaction and fulfillment outside of the family context. This can contribute to a sense of individual identity and personal accomplishment.

Enhanced Financial Opportunities: With two incomes, there may be increased financial opportunities for the family. This can include investments, savings, educational pursuits, or the ability to afford certain luxuries or experiences. The financial benefits can create a greater sense of security and provide opportunities for personal and family growth.

THE KINGDOM OF CHILD REARING

Benefits & Challenges of Child Rearing: Having children is a life-changing decision that brings both incredible rewards and significant challenges. While the experience of parenthood can vary for each individual and family, here are detailed explanations of the benefits and challenges commonly associated with having children:

BENEFITS OF HAVING CHILDREN

Emotional Fulfillment and Joy: The love and bond between parents and children can bring immense joy, fulfillment, and a sense of purpose. Watching your children grow, learn, and achieve milestones can be incredibly rewarding and create lasting memories.

Parent-Child Bond: Having children allows for the formation of a unique and deep bond between parents and their offspring. The bond created through nurturing, care, and shared experiences fosters a sense of connection and emotional closeness.

Personal Growth and Development: Parenthood often leads to personal growth, as it requires individuals to develop new skills, adapt to challenges, and prioritize the needs of their children.
Being a parent can enhance qualities such as patience, resilience, and empathy.

Legacy and Continuity: Having children allows individuals to create a lasting legacy by passing on family traditions, values, and beliefs to the next generation. It provides a sense of continuity and a link to the past while shaping the future through the upbringing and values instilled in children.

Learning and Perspective: Children bring a fresh perspective to life, encouraging parents to see the world through their eyes and rekindling a sense of wonder. Parents often learn from their children, gaining insights, acquiring new knowledge, and broadening their understanding of the world.

Emotional Support in Later Life: Having children can provide emotional support and companionship in later stages of life. Adult children often become a source of support, care, and assistance for their aging parents, creating a sense of security and comfort.

CHALLENGES OF HAVING CHILDREN

Parental Responsibilities: Raising children comes with a significant level of responsibility, including meeting their physical, emotional, and educational needs. Parents must be prepared to invest time, energy, and resources into parenting, which can be demanding and require sacrifices.

Sleep Deprivation and Exhaustion: Infants and young children often require round-the-clock care, leading to sleep deprivation and physical exhaustion for parents. Balancing the demands of parenting with other responsibilities can be challenging, especially during the early years.

Financial Considerations: Raising children can have a significant financial impact, including expenses related to healthcare, education, childcare, and general upbringing. Parents must plan and budget accordingly to provide for their children's needs and ensure their well-being.

Impact on Career and Personal Time: Balancing parenthood with career aspirations and personal time can be a juggling act. Career advancement may be affected as parents navigate work-life balance, parental leave, and the need for flexible schedules.

Emotional and Mental Strain: Parenthood can bring emotional and mental challenges, including feelings of anxiety, guilt, and self-doubt. Parenting requires navigating various stages and developmental challenges, which can be emotionally demanding.

Impact on Relationships: Having children can impact the dynamics and time available for relationships with a partner, family, and friends. Maintaining a healthy balance between parental responsibilities and nurturing other relationships requires conscious effort and communication.

It's important to note that the benefits and challenges of having children can vary greatly depending on individual circumstances, support systems, and personal preferences. Parenthood is a unique journey that brings both immense joy and significant challenges, requiring continuous adaptation, love, and dedication.

DISADVANTAGES OF HAVING CHILDREN TOO EARLY: Having children too early in life can come with several disadvantages, both for the parents and the children involved. While every situation is unique, here are some commonly recognized drawbacks:

Limited educational and career opportunities: Becoming a parent at a young age often disrupts educational pursuits. Teen parents, for example, may struggle to complete their high school or college education, limiting their career prospects. This can result in lower earning potential and financial instability for both the parent and the child.

Emotional and psychological challenges: Early parenthood can place significant emotional and psychological stress on young parents. They may be unprepared to handle the responsibilities and pressures of raising a child, which can lead to feelings of inadequacy, stress, and a sense of being overwhelmed. This can impact their mental health and well-being.

Financial difficulties: Raising a child requires financial resources, and young parents may face significant financial challenges due to their limited earning potential. They may struggle to provide for their child's needs, such as housing, food, healthcare, and education. Financial stress can strain relationships and hinder the overall well-being of the family.

Limited personal development and freedom: Having children early can restrict personal growth and limit opportunities for self-discovery. Young parents may miss out on experiences, such as travel, further education, or pursuing personal goals and ambitions. The responsibilities of parenthood can make it difficult to prioritize personal aspirations and explore one's own interests fully.

Strained relationships and support networks: Young parents may face challenges in maintaining their relationships and social connections. Their peers may be focused on different priorities, such as education or personal development, leading to feelings of isolation or disconnect. The lack of a strong support network can make parenting more challenging and overwhelming.

Increased risk of health complications: Pregnancy and childbirth at a young age can carry higher risks for both the mother and the child. Young mothers may have inadequate prenatal care, which can lead to health complications during pregnancy. Additionally, teenagers have higher rates of preterm births and low birth weights, which can impact the child's health and development.

Potential impact on child development: Children born to young parents may face certain challenges in their development. The parents' limited life experience, emotional maturity, and financial resources can impact the quality of parenting and the child's overall well-being. There may be a higher likelihood of inadequate parenting practices, such as inconsistent discipline or a lack of emotional support.

It is important to note that while early parenthood comes with its challenges, many young parents successfully navigate these difficulties and raise healthy and happy children. Supportive environments, access to education, and strong social networks can play a crucial role in mitigating some of the disadvantages associated with having children too early in life.

THE KINGDOM OF WORK-LIFE BALANCE

Work-Life Balance: Work-life balance refers to the equilibrium or harmony between one's professional commitments and personal life. It involves effectively managing the demands of work while also prioritizing and dedicating time to personal pursuits, relationships, self-care, and leisure activities. Here are detailed explanations of work-life balance:

Setting Boundaries: Establish clear boundaries between work and personal life. Define specific working hours and strive to maintain separation between work-related tasks and personal activities. Communicate your boundaries to colleagues, supervisors, and clients, making it clear when you are available and when you are not.

Time Management and Prioritization: Effectively manage your time by prioritizing tasks and responsibilities. Identify and focus on high-priority tasks that align with your goals and values. Avoid overcommitting and learn to say "no" when necessary to prevent overwhelming yourself with excessive work demands.

Flexible Work Arrangements: Explore and negotiate flexible work arrangements, such as remote work, flextime, compressed workweeks, or job-sharing.

These options can provide greater control over your schedule and allow for a better work-life balance.

Regular Breaks and Vacations: Take regular breaks throughout the workday to recharge and rejuvenate. Short breaks can improve focus, productivity, and overall well-being. Utilize your vacation time and plan for extended breaks or holidays to fully disconnect from work and engage in leisure activities, spending quality time with loved ones, or pursuing personal interests.

Effective Communication and Delegation: Communicate openly and effectively with colleagues and supervisors about your workload, deadlines, and potential challenges. Seek support or delegate tasks when necessary to prevent burnout and maintain a manageable workload.

Self-Care and Well-being: Prioritize self-care activities to promote physical and mental well-being. This can include regular exercise, sufficient sleep, healthy eating habits, relaxation techniques, and engaging in hobbies or activities that bring you joy and fulfillment.

Boundaries with Technology: Establish boundaries with technology to avoid constant connectivity and the blurring of work and personal life. Set designated times to check and respond to work-related communications, and try to disconnect during non-working hours to focus on personal time and relationships.

Quality Time with Loved Ones: Dedicate meaningful time to nurture relationships with family, friends, and loved ones. Plan activities together, engage in quality conversations, and create shared experiences that strengthen connections and support your well-being.

Reflect and Reassess Regularly: Regularly assess your work-life balance and make adjustments as needed. Recognize when the balance feels off and take proactive steps to address any imbalances. Remember, work-life balance may vary depending on individual circumstances, career choices, and personal preferences. It is about finding a balance that works for you, allowing you to meet professional obligations while also enjoying a fulfilling personal life. It requires ongoing effort, self-awareness, and a commitment to prioritizing your well-being and the various aspects of your life that bring you happiness and fulfillment.

THE KINGDOM OF LIFE COACHING

The Value of Life Coaching: Life coaching is a transformative process that empowers individuals to maximize their potential, achieve their goals, and live fulfilling lives. The value of life coaching lies in its ability to provide guidance, support, and accountability to help individuals navigate challenges, make positive changes, and unlock their true potential. Here are detailed explanations of the value of life coaching:

Clarity and Goal Setting: Life coaching helps individuals gain clarity about their values, passions, and aspirations. It supports them in setting meaningful and achievable goals aligned with their authentic desires. Coaches use various tools and techniques to help clients explore their values, assess their strengths and weaknesses, and create a vision for their ideal life.

Personal Growth and Self-awareness: Life coaching facilitates personal growth by encouraging self-reflection and self-awareness. Coaches help clients uncover limiting beliefs, patterns, and behaviors that may be holding them back from reaching their full potential. Through deep questioning and active listening, coaches help individuals gain insights into themselves, their motivations, and their barriers, enabling them to make positive changes and develop new perspectives.

Support and Accountability: Coaches provide a supportive and non-judgmental space for individuals to explore their goals, challenges, and aspirations. They offer encouragement, validation, and empathy, creating a trusting relationship that fosters growth. Coaches hold clients accountable for taking action towards their goals, providing structure and accountability to help individuals stay focused and motivated.

Problem-solving and Decision-making: Life coaching equips individuals with effective problem-solving and decision-making skills. Coaches help clients analyze challenges, explore different perspectives, and develop strategies to overcome obstacles. By facilitating the exploration of alternatives and potential consequences, coaches empower individuals to make informed decisions aligned with their values and long-term vision.

Building Confidence and Resilience: Life coaching supports individuals in building confidence, self-belief, and resilience. Coaches help clients recognize and leverage their strengths, celebrate successes, and learn from setbacks. Through personalized feedback, encouragement, and mindset-shifting techniques, coaches help individuals develop a positive mindset and the resilience to bounce back from setbacks and challenges.

Improved Relationships and Communication: Life coaching enhances interpersonal skills and communication abilities. Coaches provide tools and strategies to improve relationships, set boundaries, and enhance conflict resolution skills. By increasing self-awareness and empathy, individuals can foster deeper connections, improve communication dynamics, and create healthier and more fulfilling relationships.

Work-Life Balance: Life coaching addresses work-life balance, helping individuals align their priorities and make conscious choices to create a harmonious and fulfilling life. Coaches assist in setting boundaries, managing time effectively, and creating a sense of equilibrium between personal and professional pursuits.

Increased Motivation and Focus: Life coaching boosts motivation and focus by helping individuals tap into their intrinsic drivers and align their actions with their values and aspirations. Coaches provide strategies and tools to overcome procrastination, increase productivity, and stay focused on what matters most.

Sustainable Change and Lasting Results: Life coaching promotes sustainable change by helping individuals develop new habits, behaviors, and mindsets. Coaches provide ongoing support and guidance to ensure that the changes implemented during coaching continue to yield lasting results beyond the coaching relationship.

Personal Fulfillment and Happiness: Ultimately, life coaching enables individuals to live a life of personal fulfillment and happiness. By gaining clarity, setting meaningful goals, and making positive changes, individuals can create a life that aligns with their values, passions, and purpose. Life coaching is a collaborative process that empowers individuals to take ownership of their lives, overcome challenges, and create positive change. It provides individuals with the tools, support.

THE KINGDOM OF BUSINESS CONSULTING

Value of Career & Business Consulting: Career coaching and business consulting are valuable professional services that offer guidance, support, and expertise in navigating career and business-related challenges. They provide individuals and organizations with insights, strategies, and practical advice to enhance performance, achieve goals, and make informed decisions. Here is a more detailed explanation of the value of career coaching and business consulting:

Clarity and Direction: Career coaching helps individuals gain clarity about their career goals, aspirations, and values. Coaches assist in identifying strengths, interests, and areas for development to align career choices with personal values and aspirations. Business consultants help organizations clarify their vision, mission, and strategic goals, providing a roadmap for success.

Goal Setting and Planning: Career coaches help individuals set meaningful and achievable career goals. They guide clients in developing action plans and strategies to reach those goals, breaking them down into manageable steps. Business consultants assist organizations in setting strategic objectives and developing action plans to optimize performance and growth.

Skills Development and Enhancement: Career coaching supports individuals in developing and enhancing their skills, both technical and soft skills. Coaches provide guidance on acquiring new skills, improving existing ones, and staying relevant in a rapidly changing job market. Business consultants help organizations identify skill gaps, design training programs, and facilitate skill development initiatives for employees.

Personal and Professional Growth: Career coaching focuses on personal and professional growth, supporting individuals in overcoming obstacles and maximizing their potential. Coaches provide guidance on self-improvement, building confidence, and enhancing self-awareness. Business consultants help organizations foster a culture of learning and development, empowering employees to grow and excel in their roles.

Networking and Relationship Building: Career coaching helps individuals develop effective networking strategies, build professional relationships, and leverage connections. Coaches offer advice on building a professional network, engaging in informational interviews, and utilizing online platforms for career advancement. Business consultants assist organizations in establishing and nurturing relationships with clients, partners, and stakeholders to drive business growth.

Decision-Making Support: Career coaching provides guidance and support in making important career-related decisions. Coaches help individuals assess options, weigh pros and cons, and make informed choices aligned with their goals and values. Business consultants offer objective insights and data-driven analysis to support decision-making in various business areas, such as marketing, operations, or finance.

Performance Improvement: Career coaching supports individuals in enhancing their performance at work. Coaches help identify barriers to success, develop strategies to overcome them, and offer accountability and feedback to drive improvement. Business consultants assist organizations in identifying operational inefficiencies, optimizing processes, and implementing performance improvement initiatives.

Business Growth and Strategy: Business consulting provides organizations with expertise and guidance to drive growth and achieve strategic objectives. Consultants analyze market trends, competitive landscapes, and industry dynamics to develop effective business strategies. They offer recommendations on market entry, product development, operational efficiency, and other critical aspects of business success.

Problem-Solving and Innovation: Career coaching and business consulting foster problem-solving skills and encourage innovative thinking. Coaches and consultants help individuals and organizations approach challenges from different perspectives, explore creative solutions, and overcome barriers to success.

Accountability and Support: Career coaches and business consultants provide accountability and support throughout the process. They offer a confidential and non-judgmental space for individuals and organizations to discuss challenges, reflect on progress, and receive constructive feedback. Coaches and consultants act as trusted partners, providing motivation, encouragement, and guidance on the journey towards achieving career and business goals.

THE KINGDOM OF LEGACY

The Value of Building a Legacy: A legacy refers to the impact, influence, and imprint a person leaves behind in the world after they are gone. It encompasses the values, beliefs, accomplishments, and contributions that shape and define an individual's lasting presence. Here is a more detailed explanation of what a legacy entails:

Values and Beliefs: A legacy is built upon the values, principles, and beliefs that an individual holds dear and actively promotes. It includes the moral compass that guides their actions, decision-making, and interactions with others. These values and beliefs can be passed down through generations, shaping the behavior and mindset of their descendants.

Accomplishments and Contributions: A person's legacy is often associated with their achievements, accomplishments, and contributions in various domains of life. It can include professional successes, artistic creations, scientific advancements, philanthropic endeavors, or significant social impact. These accomplishments can inspire others and leave a mark on society, creating a lasting impression of the individual's influence.

Impact on Others: A key aspect of a legacy is the impact an individual has on the lives of others. It includes the positive influence, inspiration, and guidance they provide to family, friends, colleagues, and the wider community. A person's legacy can be seen in the lives they touch, the relationships they nurture, and the ways in which they empower and uplift others.

Family and Descendants: Legacy often extends to the family and descendants of an individual. It includes the traditions, values, stories, and memories passed down from one generation to the next. Through their actions and teachings, individuals shape the character and identity of their family lineage, leaving a lasting legacy for future generations.

Cultural and Historical Impact: Some legacies transcend personal spheres and have a broader cultural or historical significance. Individuals who make groundbreaking discoveries, contribute to the arts, champion social causes, or drive societal change leave a legacy that impacts the larger world. Their work and influence can shape the course of history, inspire movements, and leave a lasting impact on future generations.

Intellectual and Ideological Contributions: A legacy can also involve intellectual and ideological contributions. It includes the ideas, philosophies, and knowledge shared by individuals through their writings, teachings, or thought leadership. These contributions can influence academic fields, shape intellectual discourse, and foster advancements in various domains of knowledge.

Symbolic Representation: A legacy can take on symbolic representation through symbols, monuments, institutions, or legacies of honor. It may include dedications, memorials, or establishments that serve as enduring reminders of an individual's impact and influence. Creating a meaningful legacy requires intentional actions, choices, and a focus on values that align with one's vision for their impact on the world. It involves living a life of purpose, making a difference in the lives of others, and leaving a positive imprint that outlasts one's physical presence. Ultimately, a legacy reflects the essence of who an individual is, what they stand for, and how they have positively influenced the world around them.

THE 6TH JEWEL:
SPIRITUAL GROWTH

Spiritual growth refers to the process of expanding one's spiritual awareness, perspective, and connection. It involves developing a deeper understanding of oneself and the larger universe. Here is a thorough exploration of how spiritual growth impacts building a meaningful kingdom:

Self-Exploration and Self-Awareness: Spiritual growth begins with self-exploration and self-awareness. It involves reflecting on one's beliefs, values, and life purpose. Through introspection and self-reflection, individuals gain insight into their true nature, strengths, weaknesses, and areas for growth.

Connection with Something Greater: Spiritual growth often involves cultivating a sense of connection with something greater than oneself. This can include connecting with a higher power, the universe, nature, or the collective consciousness. It encompasses exploring one's spirituality, seeking meaning and purpose beyond material existence.

Developing Inner Peace and Serenity: Spiritual growth aims to cultivate inner peace, serenity, and a sense of calm. It involves practices such as meditation, mindfulness, and contemplation to quiet the mind and find stillness within. Through these practices, individuals can reduce stress, anxiety, and find a sense of inner balance and harmony.

Cultivating Compassion and Empathy: Spiritual growth involves developing compassion and empathy towards oneself and others. It entails fostering a deep understanding and acceptance of the human experience and the interconnectedness of all beings. By cultivating compassion, individuals can develop a greater capacity for love, kindness, and understanding.

Seeking Wisdom and Seeking Truth: Spiritual growth often involves seeking wisdom and truth beyond surface-level knowledge. It can include exploring philosophical, religious, or spiritual teachings to gain insight into the nature of existence, consciousness, and reality. Through seeking wisdom, individuals can broaden their perspectives, challenge assumptions, and deepen their understanding of the world.

Practicing Mindfulness and Presence: Spiritual growth involves cultivating mindfulness and presence in daily life. It entails being fully present in the present moment, observing and experiencing life without judgment or attachment. By practicing mindfulness, individuals can deepen their connection with themselves, others, and the world around them.

Embracing Personal Growth and Transformation: Spiritual growth often involves embracing personal growth and transformation. It includes recognizing and working through limiting beliefs, patterns, and behaviors that hinder personal development. By embracing growth and transformation, individuals can expand their consciousness, evolve as individuals, and align with their true potential.

Finding Meaning and Purpose: Spiritual growth involves seeking and finding meaning and purpose in life. It entails exploring one's values, passions, and desires to live a purpose-driven life. By aligning one's actions and choices with their deepest values and sense of purpose, individuals can experience a greater sense of fulfillment and satisfaction.

Practicing Gratitude and Appreciation: Spiritual growth involves cultivating gratitude and appreciation for the blessings and experiences of life. It entails acknowledging and expressing gratitude for the present moment, as well as for the lessons and growth that challenges bring. By practicing gratitude, individuals can shift their perspective, cultivate a positive mindset, and invite more joy and abundance into their lives.

Integration and Application in Daily Life: Spiritual growth is not limited to isolated practices or experiences but is integrated into daily life. It involves applying spiritual principles, values, and insights in relationships, work, and various aspects of life. By integrating spirituality into daily life, individuals can experience a more meaningful, authentic, and fulfilling existence. Spiritual growth is a personal and individual journey, and the path to growth typically is gradual and steady.

THE KINGDOM OF RELIGIOUS PRACTICE

Religious Practice: Religious practice encompasses a wide range of rituals, beliefs, and activities associated with a specific faith or belief system. Engaging in religious practice can offer numerous benefits on different levels—individual, social, and psychological. Here are some detailed benefits of religious practice:

Meaning and Purpose: Religious practice provides individuals with a sense of meaning and purpose in life. It offers a framework for understanding the purpose of existence, the nature of the universe, and one's role within it. The teachings and doctrines of a religion can guide individuals in finding purpose, direction, and a sense of belonging.

Moral and Ethical Framework: Religious practices often emphasize moral and ethical values. They provide a set of guidelines and principles that promote virtuous behavior, compassion, and respect for others. Religious teachings can offer individuals a moral compass, helping them navigate ethical dilemmas and make choices aligned with their values.

Community and Social Connection: Religious practices foster a sense of community and social connection. Places of worship, religious gatherings, and rituals provide opportunities for individuals to come together, share experiences, and support one another. Religious communities often offer a sense of belonging, emotional support, and a network of social connections.

Emotional Well-Being: Religious practices can contribute to emotional well-being and psychological resilience. They offer rituals and practices that promote inner peace, comfort, and solace during times of difficulty or grief. Prayer, meditation, and spiritual contemplation provide individuals with tools to manage stress, find emotional stability, and cultivate a sense of hope and optimism.

Health and Wellness: Religious practice has been associated with various health benefits. Studies have shown that religious individuals tend to have lower rates of certain health conditions, such as depression, anxiety, and substance abuse. Engaging in religious practices that promote healthy behaviors, such as regular exercise, abstaining from harmful substances, and practicing self-care, can contribute to overall physical and mental well-being.

Coping with Adversity: Religious practices offer individuals coping mechanisms and a source of strength during challenging times. Faith and religious beliefs can provide comfort, hope, and resilience in the face of adversity, loss, or uncertainty. Religious communities often provide support systems, counseling services, and resources to help individuals navigate difficult life events.

Rituals and Symbolism: Religious practices involve rituals, ceremonies, and symbolic acts that hold personal and cultural significance. These rituals can provide a sense of order, structure, and continuity in life, marking important milestones and transitions. Rituals and symbolism can evoke a sense of reverence, awe, and connection with something greater than oneself.

Personal Growth and Self-Reflection: Religious practices encourage personal growth and self-reflection. They offer opportunities for introspection, self-examination, and spiritual development. Through prayer, meditation, and study of religious texts, individuals can deepen their self-awareness, cultivate virtues, and strive for personal transformation.

Hope and Resilience: Religious practice can foster a sense of hope and resilience in the face of challenges and adversity. Belief in a higher power, divine providence, or a greater purpose can provide individuals with hope and optimism. Religious teachings often emphasize the concept of faith, trust, and the belief that challenges can be overcome with divine guidance and support.

Transcendent Experience: Religious practice offers opportunities for transcendent experiences, moments of connection with the divine or the sacred. These experiences can be deeply transformative, providing individuals with a sense of awe, wonder, and a glimpse into something beyond.

THE KINGDOM OF GROUP FELLOWSHIP

Group Fellowship: Group fellowship refers to the gathering and interaction of individuals within a community or organization. It offers numerous benefits and enriches the lives of participants in various ways. Here are some detailed benefits of group fellowship:

Social Support and Belonging: Group fellowship provides a sense of belonging and acceptance. It creates a supportive environment where individuals can connect with like-minded people, form friendships, and build relationships. Being part of a group can alleviate feelings of loneliness and isolation, fostering a sense of connection and social support.

Emotional Well-Being: Group fellowship contributes to emotional well-being by providing opportunities for emotional expression and validation.   Sharing experiences, challenges, and triumphs with others in a safe and non-judgmental space can help individuals process their emotions and find comfort. The empathy, understanding, and encouragement received from fellow group members can enhance emotional resilience and reduce stress.

Personal Growth and Development: Group fellowship offers a platform for personal growth and development. Interacting with diverse individuals within the group exposes individuals to different perspectives, ideas, and experiences, broadening their horizons and fostering personal growth. Group members can inspire and motivate one another, offering guidance, feedback, and constructive criticism for self-improvement.

Shared Learning and Knowledge Exchange: Group fellowship provides opportunities for shared learning and knowledge exchange. Within a group, individuals can share their expertise, skills, and experiences, creating a dynamic learning environment. Learning from others' perspectives and experiences can expand one's knowledge base, encourage critical thinking, and promote intellectual stimulation.

Mutual Accountability and Encouragement: Group fellowship encourages mutual accountability and support. Members hold each other accountable for personal goals, commitments, and behavior, fostering a sense of responsibility and motivation. The support and encouragement received from fellow group members can help individuals stay focused, motivated, and committed to their endeavors.

Skill Development and Collaboration: Group fellowship provides opportunities for skill development and collaboration. Working together within a group setting allows individuals to develop teamwork, communication, and leadership skills. Collaborative projects and activities within the group can promote creativity, problem-solving, and the exchange of ideas.

Cultural and Diversity Appreciation: Group fellowship exposes individuals to diverse cultures, backgrounds, and perspectives. Engaging with individuals from different walks of life enhances cultural awareness, promotes tolerance, and fosters appreciation for diversity. Learning about and respecting different viewpoints within the group can broaden one's understanding of the world and promote inclusivity.

Celebration and Joy: Group fellowship provides opportunities for celebration, joy, and shared experiences. Celebrating milestones, achievements, and special occasions within the group creates a sense of unity, happiness, and a shared sense of accomplishment. The collective joy experienced within the group can enhance overall well-being and create lasting memories.

Networking and Opportunities: Group fellowship offers networking opportunities and access to a broader community. Being part of a group allows individuals to expand their social and professional networks, opening doors to new opportunities, collaborations, and resources. Members can share information, contacts, and resources, creating a mutually beneficial environment for personal and professional growth.

Sense of Purpose and Impact: Group fellowship can provide individuals with a sense of purpose and the opportunity to make a positive impact. Collaborating within a group towards a common goal or shared mission can instill a sense of purpose and meaning. Working collectively towards a greater cause or serving the community can create a sense of fulfillment, satisfaction, and a feeling of making a difference. Overall, group fellowship offers numerous benefits, including social support.

THE KINGDOM OF MEDITATION

Benefits of Meditation: Meditation is a practice that involves focusing the mind, achieving a state of inner calm, and cultivating awareness. It has been practiced for centuries and has gained popularity due to its many benefits. Here are some detailed benefits of meditation:

Stress Reduction: Meditation is known for its ability to reduce stress levels. It promotes relaxation by calming the mind and body, reducing the production of stress hormones like cortisol. Regular meditation practice can help individuals manage daily stressors, enhance resilience, and improve overall well-being.

Improved Emotional Well-Being: Meditation cultivates emotional well-being by increasing self-awareness and emotional regulation. It allows individuals to observe their thoughts and emotions without judgment, leading to a greater understanding and acceptance of their internal experiences. Regular practice can reduce symptoms of anxiety, depression, and enhance emotional stability, positivity, and happiness.

Increased Focus and Concentration: Meditation enhances focus and concentration by training the mind to stay present and redirecting attention when it wanders. It strengthens the ability to sustain attention on a chosen object or task, leading to improved productivity and performance. Regular meditation practice can enhance cognitive abilities, memory, and overall mental clarity.

Mind-Body Connection: Meditation promotes a deeper connection between the mind and body. By directing attention inward, individuals become more attuned to bodily sensations, emotions, and physical well-being. This heightened awareness can help individuals detect and address early signs of physical discomfort or illness, leading to better self-care and overall health.

Improved Sleep Quality: Meditation can improve sleep quality and alleviate insomnia symptoms. It promotes relaxation and helps calm the mind, making it easier to fall asleep and reducing nighttime disturbances. Regular practice can establish a healthy sleep routine and contribute to overall sleep hygiene.

Enhanced Self-Reflection and Insight: Meditation facilitates self-reflection and introspection, allowing individuals to gain deeper insights into themselves and their experiences. It provides a space for individuals to explore their thoughts, beliefs, and values, leading to a greater understanding of themselves and their life's purpose. Regular practice can promote personal growth, self-discovery, and the development of wisdom.

Reduced Anxiety and Improved Mental Health: Meditation has been found to be effective in reducing anxiety symptoms and managing anxiety disorders. It helps individuals become more aware of anxious thoughts and sensations, allowing them to respond in a more balanced and mindful manner. Regular practice can improve overall mental health, reduce symptoms of anxiety and related disorders, and promote a sense of calm and well-being.

Increased Compassion and Empathy: Meditation cultivates compassion and empathy towards oneself and others. By developing a greater sense of self-awareness and inner calm, individuals can better understand the experiences and emotions of others. Regular practice can lead to increased kindness, empathy, and a greater ability to connect with and support others.

Enhanced Resilience and Stress Management: Meditation improves resilience by equipping individuals with tools to cope with stress and adversity. It helps individuals develop a more balanced perspective, respond to challenges with greater clarity and composure, and bounce back from setbacks. Regular practice can enhance resilience, allowing individuals to navigate life's ups and downs with greater ease.

Spiritual Growth and Transcendence: Meditation is often associated with spiritual growth and transcendence. It provides a pathway to connect with something greater than oneself, whether it be a higher power, the universe, or a sense of interconnectedness. Regular practice can deepen one's spiritual experience, foster a sense of awe and wonder, and support personal growth.

THE KINGDOM OF YOGA

The Value of Yoga: Yoga is a holistic practice that originated in ancient India and has evolved over thousands of years. It encompasses physical postures (asanas), breathing exercises (pranayama), meditation, and ethical principles. The word "yoga" comes from the Sanskrit root "yuj," which means to unite or join. It aims to create harmony and balance between the body, mind, and spirit. Here is a more detailed explanation of what yoga entails:

Physical Asanas: Yoga includes a wide range of physical postures or asanas. These postures are designed to promote strength, flexibility, balance, and body awareness. Each asana has specific benefits for different parts of the body, including muscles, joints, organs, and glands. Practicing asanas promotes physical health, improves posture, and increases overall vitality.

Breath Control (Pranayama): Pranayama involves breath control techniques practiced during yoga. It focuses on conscious breathing patterns to enhance the flow of prana (life force energy) in the body. Pranayama techniques help regulate the breath, increase lung capacity, and improve the functioning of the respiratory system. Practicing pranayama calms the mind, reduces stress, and promotes mental clarity.

Meditation and Mindfulness: Yoga includes various meditation techniques to cultivate mindfulness and inner awareness. Meditation involves focusing the mind and directing attention inward, often on a specific object, breath, or mantra. Regular meditation practice enhances concentration, reduces mental chatter, and promotes a sense of calm and clarity. It helps individuals develop a deeper understanding of their thoughts, emotions, and the nature of their mind.

Ethical Principles (Yamas and Niyamas): Yoga incorporates ethical principles known as yamas (restraints) and niyamas (observances). Yamas include principles such as non-violence (ahimsa), truthfulness (satya), non-stealing (asteya), non-excess (brahmacharya), and non-possessiveness (aparigraha).

Niyamas include principles such as cleanliness (saucha), contentment (santosha), self-discipline (tapas), self-study (svadhyaya), and surrender to a higher power (ishvara pranidhana).

The ethical principles of yoga guide individuals in leading a virtuous and balanced life, promoting harmony with oneself and others.

Mind-Body Connection and Energy Flow: Yoga emphasizes the connection between the mind and body. Practicing yoga postures and breath control techniques stimulates the flow of energy throughout the body. The energy flow, known as prana or chi, is believed to influence physical, mental, and emotional well-being. By harmonizing the mind and body, yoga helps individuals experience a sense of wholeness, balance, and vitality.

Stress Reduction and Relaxation: Yoga is well-known for its stress-reducing benefits. The practice of yoga postures, breathing techniques, and meditation promotes relaxation and reduces the body's stress response. Regular practice helps individuals manage stress, release tension, and promote a state of calm and relaxation.

Flexibility and Strength: Yoga postures improve flexibility and strength in the body. The asanas target different muscle groups, promoting flexibility, and enhancing the range of motion in the joints. Additionally, yoga postures that require balancing and holding poses build strength and stability in the muscles.

Improved Posture and Alignment: Yoga practice emphasizes proper alignment and posture. Regular practice helps.

THE KINGDOM OF SELF-REALIZATION

What is Self-Realization? Self-realization refers to the process of discovering, understanding, and actualizing one's true nature, potential, and purpose. It involves gaining deep insight into oneself, transcending limiting beliefs and conditioning, and awakening to one's innermost essence. Here is a more detailed explanation of what self-realization entails:

Self-Exploration and Self-Awareness: Self-realization begins with a journey of self-exploration and self-awareness. It involves examining one's thoughts, emotions, beliefs, values, and behaviors to gain a deeper understanding of oneself. Through introspection, self-reflection, and mindfulness, individuals become aware of their conditioned patterns, biases, and limitations.

Transcending Ego Identification: Self-realization involves transcending ego identification—the identification with the false self or the individual personality. It requires recognizing that one's true nature extends beyond the limited identification with the physical body, thoughts, and emotions. By disidentifying with the ego, individuals realize their connection to something greater, often referred to as the higher self, spirit, or consciousness.

Awakening to Inner Essence: Self-realization involves awakening to one's inner essence, which is beyond the surface-level identities and roles. It is the recognition of the timeless and eternal aspect of oneself—the essence that is beyond the transient nature of thoughts, emotions, and circumstances. This awakening brings a deep sense of peace, freedom, and a profound shift in one's perception of oneself and the world.

Aligning with Authenticity and Purpose: Self-realization entails aligning with one's authenticity and discovering one's true purpose. It involves uncovering and honoring one's innate talents, passions, and values. When individuals realize their authentic selves, they live in alignment with their deepest values, aspirations, and a sense of calling or mission.

Cultivating Inner Wisdom and Intuition: Self-realization involves accessing and cultivating inner wisdom and intuition. By quieting the mind, individuals can tap into their intuitive intelligence, which goes beyond logical reasoning and conventional knowledge. Intuition becomes a guiding force, assisting individuals in making aligned decisions and navigating life's challenges with clarity and discernment.

Liberation from Suffering and Limiting Beliefs: Self-realization leads to liberation from suffering and the transcendence of limiting beliefs. Through self-inquiry and self-awareness, individuals can identify and release deeply ingrained patterns of suffering, such as fear, attachment, and self-judgment. The realization of one's true nature brings about a sense of inner peace, contentment, and freedom from the mental and emotional constraints that cause suffering.

Integration of Mind, Body, and Spirit: Self-realization involves the integration of mind, body, and spirit. It emphasizes the interconnectedness and harmony of these aspects of the self. By recognizing the interplay between thoughts, emotions, physical sensations, and spiritual aspects, individuals experience a sense of wholeness and unity.

Cultivating Presence and Mindfulness: Self-realization involves cultivating presence and mindfulness in daily life. It emphasizes being fully present in the present moment, free from the distractions of the past or future. Mindfulness practices, such as meditation, help individuals develop a deepened awareness of the present moment and the inner workings of the mind.

Connection to Universal Consciousness: Self-realization involves recognizing the connection to universal consciousness or the divine. It is the realization that one is not separate but an integral part of the interconnected web of life. This understanding brings a sense of unity.

THE 7TH JEWEL:
PAYING IT FORWARD

"Paying it forward" is a concept that involves responding to acts of kindness or generosity by doing something kind for others, rather than reciprocating directly to the original benefactor. It's about spreading positivity and making a difference in the lives of others through selfless actions. Here is a more detailed explanation of what paying it forward entails towards building a beloved kingdom:

Acts of Kindness: Paying it forward begins with an act of kindness initiated by one person towards another. This act can take various forms, such as helping someone in need, offering assistance, giving a gift, or providing support. The act is often unexpected and comes from a place of goodwill, empathy, and a desire to make a positive impact.

Selflessness and Generosity: Paying it forward emphasizes selflessness and generosity. It goes beyond self-interest or personal gain, focusing on benefiting others without expecting anything in return. The intention behind paying it forward is to create a ripple effect of kindness, inspiring others to do the same and fostering a sense of interconnectedness and compassion.

Multiplying the Impact: The essence of paying it forward lies in multiplying the impact of kindness. Instead of repaying the original act of kindness directly, the recipient of a kind gesture extends the goodwill to others, creating a chain reaction. By passing on the kindness, the positive effects reach beyond the initial act, potentially touching the lives of numerous individuals and communities.

Inspiring Others: Paying it forward serves as an inspiration for others to engage in acts of kindness. When people witness or benefit from a selfless act, it can inspire them to participate in the cycle of giving and create their own opportunities to make a difference. The act becomes a catalyst for positive change, promoting a culture of compassion and empathy.

Cultivating Gratitude and Appreciation: Paying it forward encourages gratitude and appreciation for acts of kindness received. It prompts individuals to recognize and acknowledge the kindness they have experienced, creating a sense of gratitude for the generosity of others. By paying it forward, individuals express their appreciation by extending the kindness to others, acknowledging the positive impact it had on their own lives.

Building Stronger Communities: Paying it forward contributes to building stronger communities and fostering social connections. It creates a sense of unity and solidarity as people come together to support and uplift one another. Through acts of kindness and paying it forward, individuals create a positive social fabric that strengthens the bonds within communities.

Encouraging Empowerment: Paying it forward empowers individuals by allowing them to actively participate in creating positive change. It cultivates a sense of agency and the understanding that each person has the ability to make a difference, regardless of their resources or circumstances. By engaging in acts of kindness and paying it forward, individuals realize their capacity to impact the world positively.

Teaching Life Lessons: Paying it forward serves as a powerful tool for teaching important life lessons. It instills values such as compassion, empathy, selflessness, and gratitude in individuals. Through the act of paying it forward, people learn that even small acts of kindness can have a significant impact and that generosity has the potential to create a ripple effect of positive change.

Spreading Positivity: Paying it forward creates a culture of positivity and optimism. The selfless acts and the resulting chain reactions bring joy, hope, and happiness to individuals involved. It spreads positive energy, uplifting the overall mood and atmosphere in communities and society as a whole.

Leaving a Lasting Legacy: Leaving a lasting legacy means creating a significant and enduring impact that continues to influence and shape the world even after an individual's lifetime. It involves making a positive contribution to society, leaving behind a meaningful and lasting imprint that inspires, influences, or improves the lives of others.

THE KINGDOM OF RIGHTFUL THINKING

What is the Law of Attraction? The Law of Attraction is a concept that suggests that thoughts, beliefs, and intentions have the power to attract specific experiences, events, and circumstances into a person's life. It is based on the belief that like attracts like, and by aligning one's thoughts and emotions with their desired outcomes, they can manifest those outcomes in reality. Here is a more detailed explanation of the Law of Attraction:

Thoughts and Energy: According to the Law of Attraction, thoughts and beliefs emit a specific energy or vibration. This energy attracts similar energies or vibrations, which then manifest in corresponding experiences and events. Positive thoughts and beliefs are believed to attract positive experiences, while negative thoughts and beliefs attract negative experiences.

The Power of Intention: Intention plays a crucial role in the Law of Attraction. By setting clear and focused intentions, individuals direct their thoughts and energy towards their desired outcomes. The stronger the intention, the more likely it is to manifest in one's life.

Belief and Faith: Belief and faith are integral aspects of the Law of Attraction. It is essential to have a deep belief that what is desired can be achieved or attained. Believing in the possibility and having faith in the process allows individuals to align their thoughts and emotions with their desired outcomes.

Visualization and Affirmations: Visualization and affirmations are commonly used techniques to harness the power of the Law of Attraction. Visualization involves creating vivid mental images of the desired outcome, while affirmations are positive statements that reinforce the belief in the desired outcome. These techniques help individuals focus their thoughts and emotions on what they want to manifest, reinforcing the energy and vibration associated with their desired experiences.

Gratitude and Positive Emotions: Gratitude and positive emotions are considered powerful magnets for attracting positive experiences. Expressing gratitude for what one already has and cultivating positive emotions such as joy, love, and enthusiasm raise an individual's energetic frequency, aligning them with more positive experiences.

Mindset and Limiting Beliefs: The Law of Attraction emphasizes the importance of maintaining a positive mindset and identifying and overcoming limiting beliefs. Negative thoughts, self-doubt, and limiting beliefs can create energetic blocks and hinder the manifestation of desired outcomes. Shifting to a positive mindset and replacing limiting beliefs with empowering ones allows individuals to align their energy with their desired reality.

Taking Inspired Action: The Law of Attraction is not solely about wishful thinking or passively waiting for things to happen. Taking inspired action is a crucial element in the manifestation process. Inspired action refers to actions taken with a sense of alignment, excitement, and intuition. By taking action in line with one's desires, individuals signal their commitment and willingness to co-create their desired experiences.

Detachment and Trust: The Law of Attraction emphasizes the importance of detachment and trust in the manifestation process. Detachment means releasing the attachment to the specific how, when, and where the desired outcomes will manifest. Trusting the universe, higher power, or the process itself allows individuals to surrender control and have confidence that what is in their highest good will come to fruition.

Conscious Awareness and Responsibility: The Law of Attraction emphasizes the need for conscious awareness and taking responsibility for one's thoughts, beliefs, and emotions. Individuals are encouraged to be mindful of their internal state and make intentional choices to cultivate positive thoughts and emotions. By taking responsibility for their own experiences, individuals acknowledge their power to shape their reality.

Continuous Practice and Patience: Practicing continuous patience involves cultivating and maintaining a patient attitude and approach in various aspects of life, even in the face of challenges, delays, or frustrations. It goes beyond momentary patience and becomes an ongoing state of mind and behavior.

THE KINGDOM OF RIGHTFUL ACTION

What is the Law of Karma? The Law of Karma is a fundamental concept in various spiritual and philosophical traditions, such as Hinduism, Buddhism, and Jainism. It suggests that every action, intention, and thought has consequences that shape an individual's future experiences and circumstances. Karma is the law of cause and effect, stating that individuals reap what they sow. Here is a more detailed explanation of the Law of Karma:

Cause and Effect: The Law of Karma is based on the principle of cause and effect. It asserts that every action, whether physical, verbal, or mental, generates a corresponding outcome or consequence. Actions can be intentional or unintentional, but they all contribute to the overall karmic balance.

Intentions and Motivations: Karma places emphasis on intentions and motivations behind actions. It suggests that the quality of one's intentions influences the nature of the resulting consequences. Actions driven by positive intentions such as love, compassion, and selflessness tend to generate positive karmic effects, while actions motivated by negativity, greed, or harm generate negative karmic effects.

Accumulation and Carry-Forward: Karma is believed to accumulate over time, forming an individual's karmic "bank." Actions and choices in the past influence the present and future circumstances. Positive actions contribute to positive karmic accumulation, leading to favorable outcomes, while negative actions contribute to negative karmic accumulation, leading to unfavorable outcomes.

Interconnectedness: Karma highlights the interconnectedness of all beings and actions. It suggests that every action has an impact not only on the individual performing it but also on others and the collective consciousness. Positive actions contribute to the overall positive energy in the world, while negative actions contribute to the overall negative energy.

Reincarnation and Multiple Lifetimes: The Law of Karma is often associated with the belief in reincarnation. It suggests that the consequences of actions may extend beyond one's current lifetime. Positive or negative karmic effects accumulated in one life may influence future lives and shape the circumstances and experiences of subsequent incarnations.

Personal Responsibility: Karma emphasizes personal responsibility for one's actions, choices, and their consequences. Individuals are seen as active participants in creating their own destiny through their thoughts, words, and deeds. This encourages individuals to take ownership of their actions and make conscious choices aligned with positive values.

Learning and Growth: Karma is viewed as a mechanism for learning and growth. It is believed that individuals face the consequences of their actions to learn important life lessons, develop virtues, and evolve spiritually. Positive actions contribute to the accumulation of positive karma, fostering personal growth and facilitating the journey towards liberation or enlightenment.

Purification and Liberation: Karma serves as a means of purification and liberation from the cycle of suffering and rebirth. The ultimate goal is to attain liberation from the cycle of reincarnation and achieve spiritual enlightenment or self-realization. This is achieved by resolving and balancing one's karmic debts through righteous actions, selfless service, spiritual practice, and cultivating wisdom and compassion.

Non-Judgmental Nature: Karma is seen as a non-judgmental law. It does not imply punishment or reward but rather focuses on the consequences of actions. The purpose of karma is to provide opportunities for growth, self-reflection, and the evolution of consciousness, rather than to inflict suffering or reward.

Free Will and Course Correction: While karma suggests that actions have consequences, it also acknowledges the presence of free will. Individuals have the power to make conscious choices in spite of the effects created; choose wisely.

THE KINGDOM OF HUMAN CONNECTION

In our increasingly digital and fast-paced world, human connection holds an immeasurable importance in shaping our lives and well-being. It is a fundamental aspect of our existence that nourishes our emotional, psychological, and physical being. Human connection goes beyond mere social interaction, transcending the superficial to foster empathy, understanding, and a sense of belonging. In this article, we will explore the profound significance of human connection and its transformative power in our lives.

Enhancing Emotional Well-being: Human connection is an essential ingredient for emotional well-being. Genuine connections allow us to express and share our emotions, fostering a sense of validation and understanding. Whether it is through deep conversations, sharing experiences, or offering support during challenging times, human connection provides a safe space to be vulnerable. It helps to alleviate feelings of loneliness, anxiety, and depression, creating a sense of belonging and acceptance. When we feel heard and understood by others, our emotional resilience and overall happiness are significantly enhanced.

Fostering Empathy and Understanding: Human connection serves as a bridge that enables us to relate to others, fostering empathy and understanding. When we engage in meaningful interactions with diverse individuals, we gain valuable perspectives and insights into different cultures, backgrounds, and experiences. This broader understanding cultivates compassion, reduces prejudice, and nurtures a sense of unity in an increasingly interconnected world. Through human connection, we develop a deeper appreciation for the shared human experience, transcending boundaries and fostering a more inclusive society.

Promoting Physical Health: Studies consistently demonstrate the impact of human connection on physical health. Strong social ties have been linked to a reduced risk of developing chronic diseases, lower mortality rates, and faster recovery from illness or surgery. Meaningful relationships encourage healthy behaviors such as regular exercise, better nutrition, and improved self-care. Moreover, the emotional support gained through human connection directly influences the body's stress response, bolstering the immune system and reducing the risk of mental and physical ailments.

Enhancing Personal Growth: Human connection provides an environment conducive to personal growth and self-discovery. Through interactions with others, we learn more about ourselves, our values, and our aspirations. Meaningful relationships provide support and encouragement, empowering us to take risks, overcome challenges, and pursue our passions. Additionally, connecting with individuals who possess different perspectives and skills broadens our horizons, stimulates creativity, and inspires personal development. The guidance and mentorship received through human connection can be transformative, unlocking our full potential.

Creating a Sense of Purpose: Human connection plays a vital role in shaping our sense of purpose and meaning in life. By forming meaningful relationships and contributing to the well-being of others, we experience a sense of fulfillment that extends beyond our own individual existence. The connections we forge provide opportunities for collaboration, collective problem-solving, and shared accomplishments, fostering a sense of belonging and purpose. Through human connection, we recognize the interconnectedness of all beings and our capacity to make a positive impact on the world.

Human connection is a powerful force that enriches our lives on multiple levels. It is a reminder that we are not isolated individuals, but rather interdependent members of a greater community. Nurturing human connection through meaningful relationships and genuine interactions allows us to experience emotional well-being, empathy, physical health, personal growth, and a profound sense of purpose. In a world often characterized by distance and disconnection, let us recognize and prioritize the importance of human connection, for it is through these connections that we truly thrive as individuals and as a society.

THE KINGDOM OF QUANTUMNESS

Quantum entanglement, a phenomenon that defies classical physics, has captivated scientists and philosophers alike since its discovery. While primarily studied in the realm of quantum mechanics, there is growing speculation about the potential implications of quantum entanglement on human beings. We will delve into the fascinating world of quantum entanglement and explore how it pertains to human beings, offering intriguing insights into the nature of our interconnectedness.

Understanding Quantum Entanglement: Quantum entanglement occurs when two or more particles become intricately linked, such that their properties are instantaneously correlated, regardless of the distance between them. This means that if one particle's state is altered, its entangled partner will experience an immediate and corresponding change, even if they are light-years apart. This phenomenon challenges our conventional understanding of cause and effect and suggests an interconnectedness that transcends space and time.

The Concept of Non-Locality: Quantum entanglement suggests the existence of a non-local reality, where particles can be connected regardless of their physical separation. While this phenomenon has been observed and tested extensively in controlled laboratory settings, its extrapolation to the macroscopic world of human beings remains a topic of speculation. Some theorists propose that quantum entanglement could extend beyond the quantum realm, implying a potential interconnectedness between human beings that transcends traditional notions of proximity and distance.

Quantum Entanglement and Consciousness: The relationship between quantum entanglement and consciousness is an area of ongoing debate and exploration. Some theories suggest that consciousness, often considered a product of complex neuronal activity, could be influenced or influenced by the principles of quantum mechanics. Proponents of this idea propose that consciousness may arise from the entangled state of particles within the brain, allowing for non-local connections and information processing beyond traditional neural networks. However, it is essential to note that this is still a highly speculative and controversial area of study within the scientific community.

Quantum Entanglement and Interconnectedness: Quantum entanglement raises profound questions about the interconnectedness of all things, including human beings. If particles can be entangled and connected regardless of distance, is it possible that we, as conscious beings, are also connected in some fundamental way? The idea of interconnectedness aligns with ancient spiritual and philosophical beliefs that emphasize the interdependence of all phenomena. Quantum entanglement may provide a scientific framework to explore and potentially validate these notions of interconnectedness on a deeper level.

Practical Applications and Future Possibilities: While the direct implications of quantum entanglement on human beings are still largely speculative, there are practical applications of this phenomenon that could potentially impact our lives. Quantum entanglement forms the foundation for quantum computing, secure communication protocols, and high-precision sensing technologies. These advancements may lead to transformative developments in various fields, including healthcare, finance, and information technology, ultimately shaping the way we interact and connect with one another.

The human brain, often described as the most complex organ in the known universe, has captivated scientists and researchers for centuries. Recent advancements in neuroscience and quantum physics have given rise to a fascinating theory: the human brain may possess a quantum entangled connection to the cosmos. Quantum entanglement is a mesmerizing phenomenon that challenges our understanding of reality and opens up a realm of possibilities. While its direct connection to human beings remains a topic of exploration and debate, the concept of interconnectedness that emerges from quantum entanglement has profound philosophical, scientific, and spiritual implications. As we continue to unravel the mysteries of quantum mechanics, we may gain deeper insights into the nature of our existence, the interconnected web of life, and the potential unity that transcends physical boundaries.

THE KINGDOM OF SERVICE

The Value of Charitable Service: Charitable service, also known as volunteering or giving back, refers to selfless actions undertaken to benefit others or the community without expecting anything in return. It involves donating time, skills, or resources to support causes, organizations, or individuals in need. The value of charitable service is significant, and here are several detailed benefits it brings:

Making a Positive Impact: Charitable service allows individuals to make a direct and positive impact on the lives of others and the community. By volunteering or engaging in charitable acts, individuals can address various social, environmental, or humanitarian issues. It provides an opportunity to contribute to causes that align with personal values and passions, creating a sense of fulfillment and purpose.

Helping Those in Need: Charitable service provides assistance and support to individuals or communities facing challenges or difficult circumstances. It helps to alleviate suffering, improve quality of life, and provide necessary resources to those who are less fortunate. Whether it's volunteering at a homeless shelter, supporting disaster relief efforts, or providing education and healthcare services, charitable service helps to meet critical needs and uplift the vulnerable.

Building Stronger Communities: Engaging in charitable service fosters a sense of community and strengthens social connections. It brings people from diverse backgrounds together, promoting understanding, empathy, and solidarity. By working collectively towards a common goal, individuals develop a sense of belonging and pride in their community. Strong communities with active volunteers tend to be more resilient, cohesive, and supportive.

Personal Growth and Development: Charitable service offers opportunities for personal growth and development. Volunteering allows individuals to develop and enhance various skills, such as leadership, teamwork, communication, and problem-solving. It provides a platform for learning about different cultures, perspectives, and social issues, fostering personal growth, empathy, and tolerance. Engaging in charitable activities also boosts self-confidence, provides a sense of accomplishment, and broadens one's horizons.

Building Networks and Relationships: Charitable service creates avenues to meet new people and build meaningful relationships. Working alongside like-minded individuals who share a passion for a cause can lead to long-lasting friendships and professional connections. Volunteering often brings together people from diverse backgrounds, facilitating the exchange of ideas, experiences, and knowledge.

Enhancing Well-being and Health: Engaging in charitable service has been linked to improved physical and mental well-being. It can reduce stress levels, combat feelings of loneliness or isolation, and provide a sense of purpose and fulfillment. Helping others has been shown to release endorphins, the "feel-good" hormones, promoting a positive mood and overall happiness.

Inspiring Others: Charitable service acts as a powerful catalyst for inspiring others to get involved and make a difference. By leading by example, individuals who engage in charitable acts motivate and encourage others to contribute their time, skills, or resources. This ripple effect can create a significant collective impact and promote a culture of giving and compassion in society.

Strengthening Social Responsibility: Charitable service reinforces the importance of social responsibility and ethical behavior. It encourages individuals and organizations to actively participate in addressing societal challenges and working towards a more equitable and just world. By engaging in charitable service, individuals become aware of the needs and struggles of others, fostering a sense of social consciousness and promoting a sense of duty to contribute to the greater good.

Creating Long-Term Sustainable Change: Charitable service is not only about immediate assistance but also about creating long-term sustainable change. Through volunteering, advocacy, or philanthropy, individuals can support initiatives.

THE KINGDOM OF REWARD

The Joy of Helping Others: The experience of joy when helping others is a complex phenomenon that involves various psychological, neurological, and social processes. While the exact mechanisms are still being studied, several scientific theories and findings shed light on the science behind this joy:

Neurobiology of Reward: Helping others activates brain regions associated with the experience of pleasure and reward. When individuals engage in acts of kindness or charitable behavior, the brain releases neurotransmitters such as dopamine, serotonin, and oxytocin, which are associated with positive emotions, well-being, and social bonding. These neurochemicals contribute to feelings of happiness, satisfaction, and a sense of reward.

Social Connection and Empathy: Humans are social beings, and our brains are wired to connect with others and experience empathy. When helping others, the brain's empathy networks are activated, allowing individuals to understand and resonate with the experiences and emotions of those they are assisting. Empathetic responses trigger feelings of compassion, leading to a desire to alleviate suffering and promote well-being in others. These empathetic responses are linked to the release of oxytocin, often referred to as the "bonding hormone," which strengthens social bonds and fosters positive emotions.

Altruism and Evolutionary Benefits: Evolutionary psychologists propose that helping behavior and altruism have adaptive advantages for human survival and well-being. Engaging in prosocial acts, such as helping others, can strengthen social bonds, promote cooperation, and enhance the overall functioning of social groups. The joy experienced when helping others may be a result of evolutionary mechanisms that reward altruistic behavior, increasing the likelihood of its continuation in future generations.

Self-Transcendence and Meaning: Helping others often involves a sense of self-transcendence, where individuals move beyond their own self-interests and connect to a larger purpose or cause. Engaging in acts of kindness and making a positive impact on others can provide a sense of meaning, purpose, and fulfillment. Research suggests that experiencing meaning and purpose in life is associated with increased well-being and life satisfaction.

Psychological Benefits: Helping others has been linked to various psychological benefits, contributing to the experience of joy. Engaging in acts of kindness can increase feelings of self-worth, self-esteem, and personal competence. It can also foster a sense of gratitude and appreciation for one's own circumstances, leading to a positive outlook on life. Helping behavior can provide a sense of control and agency, as individuals actively contribute to improving the lives of others or the world around them.

Positive Social Reinforcement: Helping behavior is often met with positive social reinforcement and appreciation from others. When individuals receive gratitude, recognition, or praise for their acts of kindness, it reinforces their positive emotions and encourages continued prosocial behavior. The positive social feedback further amplifies the experience of joy and satisfaction associated with helping others.

It's important to note that the experience of joy when helping others can vary across individuals, contexts, and cultures. Additionally, the motivations and intentions behind helping behavior can influence the joy experienced. Nevertheless, the scientific understanding of the joy people experience when helping others highlights the inherent interconnectedness of human beings and the benefits of acts of kindness and compassion on individual well-being and social cohesion.

THE KINGDOM OF PHILANTHROPY

The Value of Philanthropy: The value of philanthropy extends beyond the act of giving and encompasses a range of benefits for individuals, communities, and society as a whole. Here are several detailed aspects that highlight the value of philanthropy:

Addressing Social Issues and Inequality: Philanthropy plays a crucial role in addressing societal challenges and promoting social justice. By directing resources towards critical areas such as education, healthcare, poverty alleviation, and environmental conservation, philanthropy aims to create a more equitable and sustainable world. It can help bridge gaps in access to resources and opportunities, empowering marginalized individuals and communities.

Promoting Positive Social Change: Philanthropy serves as a catalyst for positive social change by supporting innovative solutions and initiatives. It allows individuals and organizations to invest in research, advocacy, and grassroots efforts that aim to tackle pressing social, cultural, and environmental issues. Philanthropic initiatives can drive systemic change, influence policies, and shape public opinion, leading to transformative outcomes.

Strengthening Civil Society: Philanthropy contributes to the development and strengthening of civil society, fostering active citizen participation and engagement. By supporting nonprofit organizations, philanthropy helps build a vibrant and resilient civil society sector that works towards the betterment of communities. Nonprofits provide vital services, advocate for social causes, and mobilize collective action, with philanthropy serving as a key source of support.

Encouraging Innovation and Risk-Taking: Philanthropy offers resources and support for innovative ideas and projects that may not receive funding through traditional channels. It encourages risk-taking and experimentation, enabling individuals and organizations to explore new approaches and solutions to complex problems. Philanthropic investments in research, entrepreneurship, and technology can drive innovation and create positive disruptions in various fields.

Leveraging Resources and Influence: Philanthropy leverages financial resources, expertise, networks, and influence to amplify impact. Philanthropists often bring together their financial capital, knowledge, and connections to address social issues holistically. By collaborating with other stakeholders, including governments, businesses, and civil society organizations, philanthropy can mobilize collective resources and drive coordinated efforts towards common goals.

Encouraging Empathy and Social Responsibility: Philanthropy fosters empathy, compassion, and a sense of social responsibility. It encourages individuals to recognize their privilege and use their resources to make a positive difference in the lives of others. Philanthropy promotes a culture of giving and caring, inspiring others to engage in acts of kindness and contribute to the well-being of society.

Personal Fulfillment and Well-being: Engaging in philanthropy can bring personal fulfillment and a sense of purpose. Giving back and making a positive impact on others' lives can enhance well-being and life satisfaction. Philanthropy provides opportunities for individuals to align their values with their actions, fostering a sense of meaning and connection to a higher purpose.

Legacy and Intergenerational Impact: Philanthropy allows individuals to leave a lasting legacy and create intergenerational impact. By establishing foundations, endowments, or charitable trusts, individuals can ensure their philanthropic efforts continue beyond their lifetime, supporting causes they care about for years to come. Philanthropic endeavors can inspire future generations to continue the legacy of giving and contribute to positive social change.

Overall, the value of philanthropy lies in its ability to drive positive social impact, promote equity, empower communities, foster innovation, and create a more compassionate and inclusive society. It reflects the power of collective action and the potential for individuals and organizations to make meaningful and lasting changes in the world.

THE WORLD KINGDOM

In a world facing numerous challenges, both social and environmental, it is crucial that each of us takes responsibility for making a positive impact. Leaving the world a better place requires collective efforts and individual actions aimed at promoting sustainability, equality, and compassion. By incorporating certain principles into our daily lives, we can contribute to creating a brighter future for generations to come. This article explores practical steps that individuals can take to make a lasting difference.

Promoting Environmental Sustainability:
a. Reduce, Reuse, Recycle: Minimize waste by adopting a lifestyle focused on reducing consumption, reusing items whenever possible, and recycling materials. Embrace practices such as composting, water conservation, and energy efficiency to limit your environmental footprint.

b. Support Renewable Energy: Transition to clean and renewable energy sources, such as solar or wind power, in your home or workplace. Encourage the adoption of sustainable energy policies and technologies in your community.

c. Embrace Sustainable Transportation: Opt for eco-friendly modes of transportation, such as walking, cycling, or using public transit whenever feasible. Consider carpooling or driving electric vehicles to reduce emissions and congestion.

Cultivating Social Equality
a. Practice Inclusion and Diversity: Embrace diversity in all aspects of life, promoting inclusivity and equality. Challenge prejudices and biases, and actively engage in dialogue to foster understanding and empathy.

b. Support Education: Recognize the power of education in transforming lives and societies. Advocate for equal access to quality education for all, supporting initiatives that promote literacy, skills development, and lifelong learning.

c. Champion Human Rights: Stand up against injustice and human rights abuses. Support organizations that protect vulnerable communities, advocate for gender equality, and fight against discrimination in all forms.

Engaging in Compassionate Actions
a. Volunteer and Give Back: Dedicate your time, skills, or resources to help those in need. Engage in volunteer work with local charities, community

organizations, or international initiatives. Contribute to causes aligned with your passions and values.

b. Practice Kindness: Simple acts of kindness can have a profound impact on others' lives. Show compassion, empathy, and respect in your interactions with people, animals, and the environment. Small gestures can create ripples of positivity.

c. Foster Collaboration: Recognize that tackling global challenges requires collective action. Collaborate with like-minded individuals and organizations to create meaningful change. Join or initiate local initiatives addressing issues such as poverty alleviation, climate action, or community development.

Advocate for Systemic Change
a. Engage in Responsible Consumption: Support businesses and organizations that prioritize sustainability, ethical practices, and social responsibility. Be an informed consumer, choose products with minimal ecological impact, and hold corporations accountable for their actions.

b. Influence Policy: Participate in civic activities, such as voting and engaging with local and national policymakers. Voice your concerns and support policies that promote sustainable development, protect human rights, and address societal issues.

c. Raise Awareness: Utilize your voice and platforms to raise awareness about pressing global challenges.

Share knowledge, educate others, and use social media or traditional channels to advocate for change. Encourage critical thinking and inspire others to take action. Leaving the world a better place demands collective effort, but each individual's contribution is vital. By adopting sustainable practices, promoting social equality, and cultivating compassion, we can make a positive impact on our planet and its inhabitants. Let us embrace the responsibility to create a more sustainable, inclusive, and empathetic world, one small step at a time. Together, we can leave a lasting legacy of positive change for future generations.

RULING YOUR KINGDOM

In conclusion, as we journey through the realm of being a king or queen, we have explored the profound significance of the seven jewels that shape our lives. These jewels, woven together, create a tapestry of empowerment, fulfillment, and profound impact. Let us reflect on the transformative insights we have gained and embrace the essence of true royalty.

First Jewel, financial wellness has taught us the importance of mastering our kingdom of wealth. By cultivating a mindset of abundance, practicing effective budgeting and spending, creating income and savings, and managing debt, we have built a solid foundation for prosperity and financial freedom.

Second Jewel, asset ownership has bestowed upon us the power to reign over our destiny. We have learned to discern between assets and liabilities, nurturing those that appreciate and propel us forward. By harnessing the potential of real estate, investing wisely, and embracing financial planning, we have unlocked the gateways to lasting wealth and security.

Third Jewel, strategic education has enlightened us, unveiling the path to personal growth and success. We have witnessed the immeasurable value of acquiring knowledge, both formal and experiential. By seeking clever ways to gain education, embracing technical schools and certifications, we have armed ourselves with the tools to reign supreme in our chosen fields.

Fourth Jewel, healthy living has taught us that our bodies are temples deserving of reverence and care. Through mindful practices, we have woven physical fitness, nutritious diets, and self-care into the fabric of our lives. By incorporating exercise routines, nurturing our well-being, and cultivating work-life balance, we have paved the way for vitality and longevity.

Fifth Jewel, family & work-life balance has emerged as a vital jewel, reminding us to cherish our kingdom of relationships. We have learned to honor our responsibilities while nurturing our passions and nurturing our connections with loved ones. By tending to our families, cultivating meaningful friendships, and valuing quality time, we have harmonized the realms of work and personal fulfillment.

Sixth Jewel, spiritual growth has expanded our horizons, reminding us of our divine nature and connection to something greater. Through introspection, meditation, and embracing the practices of yoga and self-realization, we have deepened our understanding of ourselves and our purpose. We have discovered that true royalty lies in the depth of our spirituality and the impact it has on our lives and the lives of others.

Seventh Jewel, paying it forward has revealed the true essence of noble leadership. By practicing responsibility, accountability, and service to others, we have embraced our role as influencers and stewards of positive change. We have witnessed the profound joy that comes from giving back, leaving a lasting legacy, and uplifting those in need.

As we momentarily conclude this regal journey, let us remember that being a king or queen is not defined by external trappings or titles, but by the embodiment of these seven jewels in our lives. It is the culmination of financial wellness, asset ownership, strategic education, healthy living, family combined with work-life balance, spiritual growth, and paying it forward that makes us true royalty.

So, my fellow kings and queens, let us walk forth with heads held high, knowing that we possess the wisdom, power, and grace to create a kingdom of abundance, impact, and love. May our lives be a testament to the greatness that lies within us, and may we inspire others to discover and embrace their own regal destinies. For in the realm of metaphorical kings and queens, the potential for extraordinary transformation knows no bounds. And oh yeah, btw… **WEAR YOUR KROWN?!**

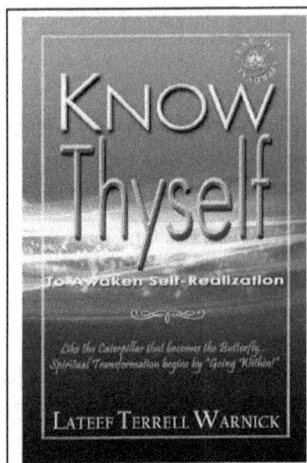

One's inner search brings the awareness and direct experience of Spirit. This is accomplished through three phases of Evolution, Experience and Enlightenment.

Evolution: The Book of Genesis symbolically represents how the world comes into being. The formless Spirit mystically descends, taking form, within creation.

Experience: Everything that we experience in this world of duality is what we call life. Through infinite possibilities, we make choices and are intended to grow and evolve but where are we going?

Enlightenment: Many take the Book of Revelation to mean "Armageddon" thus feeding fear of the end of the world. But what if hidden within these pages were secrets towards man's spiritual enlightenment?

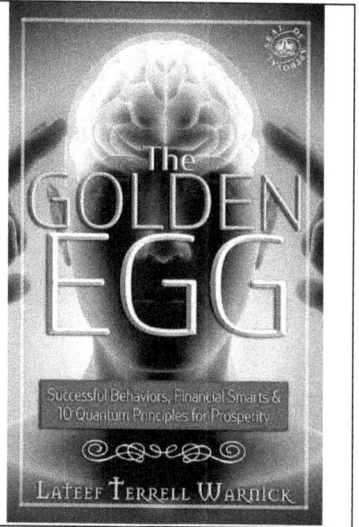

Most are familiar with the concept of karma, you reap what you sow, what goes around comes around and so on. This isn't your "bubble gum" metaphysics.

This book was written for the sincere Truth Seeker that places Self-Realization first and foremost. Upon finding the Eternal treasure within, lasting prosperity is a natural result and not merely a measure of your material possessions.

P.R.O.S.P.E.R.I.T.Y. –

"POWERFUL REASONS OPTIMISTIC SERVICE PRODUCES EXPONENTIAL RICHNESS INEVITABLY THROUGH YOU!"